MW00814871

Poems about discovering the courage to be vulnerable.

HEAR ME SING: BOOK I

Rivka A. Edery, M.S.W., L.C.S.W.

ISBN-13: 978-1530177981
ISBN-10: 1530177987

"... I can raise You on high, O God, for You have raised me from the depths and have not allowed my enemies to rejoice over me..."

PSALM 30

CONTENTS
Acknowledgments
About The Author
Introduction

ACKNOWLEDGMENTS

To Susan and Goldie
For your unconditional love.
You continue to inspire my Transformation.

To my Higher Power:
Thank you for meeting me in every place I have
visited, rescuing and supporting me with Your
Hand of love and compassion. If all the trees in the
world were pens, the oceans ink, and earth
parchment; I still could not thank You enough.

-Rivka

ABOUT THE AUTHOR

Rivka Edery is a career social worker who has ministered to scores of clients in crisis and deep emotional pain: drug addicts, mentally ill, adolescents at risk, victims of poverty, children of deployed military, and veterans in treatment for Post-Traumatic Stress Disorder. She has been on the frontline of intervention at some of the most prominent facilities and treatment centers in New York State.

Rivka is much more than a clinician, mental health writer, and researcher. She brings her enlightened soul forward to share the truths from her own healing journey that began in childhood. As a Twelve-Step veteran of twenty years, she is a true Survivor/Healer who creates a healing process in every relationship. She inspires and awakens hope in all the human beings her life touches, in whatever context.

Canadian born and daughter of a family of distinguished Rabbinical Scholars, Rivka attended grade school in Montreal and Toronto. Her first languages were French and Hebrew. When she moved to New York City in her late teens, she became independent. Self-supporting, she graduated from Thomas Edison State University, and earned her Master of Social Work degree, with a research track, from Fordham University, in New York City.

Rivka became a psychotherapist, and published her landmark book *Trauma and Transformation: A 12 Step Guide* in 2013. She clinically systematized the tools of the spiritual Twelve Steps of Alcoholics Anonymous, that had healed her own struggles with addictions, symptomatic of childhood abuse, and Complex Post-Traumatic Stress Disorder. Her book brilliantly brings into focus the spiritual dimension as an essential dynamic in healing from early childhood trauma, and addiction. The exposition of this synthesis between the spiritual tools and the clinical tools has expanded the access to the revered Twelve Step program beyond the addiction community, to P.T.S.D. patients with all types of symptoms.

Simply stated, Rivka has shown us how an individual's practice of faith in a higher power corrects pathological perspective, and can resolve psychological pain and injury. She has established herself as a professional guide into a patient's personal spiritual relationship, that can heal the inner torture of living with ongoing traumatic stress. Rivka has expanded her clinical work to include a wide network of followers on social media. Through ongoing talk radio programs and multiple groups, her evolving healing tools are continuously available to her followers.

Rivka Edery has found a new voice, that of a poet! Her work with victims of great suffering has brought her to a new level of spiritual transformation, which she invites us to experience. In her new book, *Hear Me Sing Book I*, she completely embodies her identity as a spiritual healer and becomes a psalmist. Her songs reach to guide our broken hearts. They are songs of transforming the pain of unrequited love. Rivka's poems celebrate the heart that continues to be grateful for love after rejection, for love abiding in spite of the trauma of abandonment, a love that prevails through being forsaken, that survives the obliterating cruelty of solitude. She shows us how we are never alone, as whimsical healing partners emerge in the form of Rivka's various crones, goddesses. trolls and monsters in a landscape glittering with wonders. *Hear Me Sing Book I* is a passionate recording of a beautiful heart that never stops singing and loving. There is mystery in how Rivka is able to give so much. Could it be that she allows herself to be so beloved by her God, that her spirit sings in giving that love back? Failed romantic love is the match that creates a painful fire in her soul, leading her through a spiritual journey, and building enough energy to move mountains. The pain of this poet is not that of a victim asking for mercy, but the seizing of archetypal adventure and relishing a full, joyful emotional life.

Some of Rivka's followers on-line have compared her to the ancient poet Rumi. As a long-time friend and colleague who has received these poems one by one, I am joyful that the first 100 Songs of Rivka Edery will soon be published.

With love and gratitude for your bright and beautiful voice that touches the deepest chords,
Susan Price

Hear Me Sing: Book I. Rivka A. Edery, M.S.W., L.C.S.W.

INTRODUCTION

As a young child, I loved the written and spoken word. I would magically enter the pages of a book or story, and suddenly I was no longer sitting on the chair reading it. I was transported there, and everything came alive for me. Reading and writing poems were my solace and solitude; it was my deepest joyful celebration, and my creativity gave me life. It was only during those moments that I felt most profoundly connected to my Source. I felt like I was sitting next to the most beautiful, golden fire - and at the same time, I was the Wick.

A great storm hit my life during adolescence, and I stopped writing. It has only been since March of 2015 that these poetic embers have begun burning again so fiercely. I was awakened, and inspired, by an encounter with someone in a way that I never could have imagined. This book of poems is the celebratory music and painting of my voice. They reflect the human condition - in all its joy, pain, suffering, yearnings, depth of encounters, mystery of love and relationships, and ultimately our connection with the Divine. I hope that the words of my soul will afford you an opportunity to reach deeper into yourself. Perhaps you will discover that true love begins with an open heart, and the courage to be vulnerable.

-Rivka
New York, March 2016

FEAR OF ABANDONMENT:
A SECRET SABOTAGE

Abandonment pushes the abandoned
to seek love from those
who cannot give love.

This is how abandonment issues
secretly sabotage you.

Fear of abandonment
will continue to attract
more and more people to abandon you
until you let go of the fear.

This core issue
lives in the bottom of the ocean
of our unconscious,
and is our most primitive
and basic fear.

It is the linchpin of addictions,
compulsions,
the False Self,
the Ego's motivator,
and a host of dysfunctional human behavior.

I acknowledge
both its evolutionary purpose,
and its' existence
as the Crater of Woundedness
in all of us.

1

Once I admit this
into consciousness,
I can make an effective decision
to turn away
from my False Self,
towards my Higher Self
for love, direction and resolution.

I WAS ONCE TERRIFIED

I was once terrified to love
because I could not stomach
separation
and possibility of loss.

Now I question myself:
"How can I lose
something created by me,
something that runs
through the very fabric
of my existence?"

I still fear
loss and separation,
but those are just voices
of old ghosts
trying to call me back
to their graveyard
of lies, deceit, and blindness.

I have left that place
of scarcity and desolation,
but those ghosts
want me to believe
that my new ideas about Love
cannot possibly be real and true for me.

To them I say:
"It was you
that was never real and true.
You were just
somebody else's lie."

THE GREATEST ACT OF LOVE

With each of my romantic encounters
there was an underlying purpose:
To advance my spiritual growth,
however painful or uncomfortable.

It is not revealed right away,
since clarity takes time to develop.
Or, the purpose may be accomplished
in a short time,
not always leaving room
for a proper ending.

But if we both show up,
and answer the spiritual calling
(without even knowing what we are doing),
we have committed
the greatest act of love.

That is because we were "faithful servants"
to each other's higher purpose.

To extend this Love for a stranger
is not something
modern day media on romance
teaches us.

But this may possibly be
the "true love "
we are all seeking.

4

My Ego tells me
to clutch on,
forever dictating my pain.

My Soul rejoices in knowing
that She has been walked towards home
a few steps closer
through this encounter.

<u>MY ORIGINAL WOUND</u>

My original wound
of loss and betrayal
occurred by people.
Therefore, I need people
to help me heal.
Not just anyone,
but deep, meaningful, genuine,
safe, human connections.

But since Abandonment
is my deepest fear,
(in fact,
the most powerful of all human fears);
I have tortured tension inside me,
borne of this dilemma.

It is not enough for me
to cognitively grasp
that ideas of separation
are the Ego's Smoke Screen.

My injuries exist in a place
where language, words, and cognition
cannot reach.

My heart keeps asking me
Where do I find loving, stable,
committed human connections?

I mistakenly thought
I did not need any of this,
since it reminded me too much
of the original love
that was not really love at all.

I thought I was tough enough to bypass
this empty and neglected space.

Unable to bear the pain,
I have discovered
that this hole
cannot be filled with anything
but unconditional love.

When I feel the power
of loving human connections,
I feel it in that part of my brain
that was once so open, so tender,
and so pure with love
But had been abandoned
to the darkness.

I see God's intervention
in the melting away of my armor,
And in my willingness
to accept Love as Energy
without conditions.

In this way,
all the Healers I have been blessed with
have rescued my soul.

*These are ordinary people
who loved me
without demanding in return,
delivering
a simple and ancient message.*

THE ULTIMATE MAGICIAN

All along I thought it was you,
but I just could not say it.

What if you ran and hid?
You did that already.

What if you felt rage?
judgment and rejection of me?
I know what that feels like.

What if you saw me at the deepest level?
and were indifferent?

I faced my fears,
but not by choice.
I faced them
because in you I saw
an exact emotional replica
of myself.

I thought that I was
the Ultimate Magician.

And then I met you,
and as I was busy checking
if my heart would be safe,
You had already stolen it,
and run away.

I chased after you,
along the shores of my unconscious waters.

I kept chasing you,
but like a thief on the run
with the most valuable possession,
you were gone.

I sat alone on the beach,
and cried
until my eyes could no longer weep.

I realized that you were
a manifestation of my fantasy:
that one day I would no longer be
the Ultimate Magician.

And this would happen
because I became entirely ready
to sit alone
on the great ocean of my unconscious,
and see my own reflection in you.

That is how I knew
it was you all along
that I needed and was seeking.

Now,
there are no more magicians in me.

A prayer
has replaced these magicians,
that you will not hide in lonely desperation,
for the next magician
to enable your escape
and reflect your own masks.

YOU FOREVER TAMED ME

You forever tamed me
because you asked me
something no one else did,
and forced me to go to the
ocean floor of my unconscious.

I am forever changed
because of you.

But you already know that.

And just because you did this to me,
does not mean
I will hold you responsible forever.
Graciously, I do not hold myself
responsible for you either.

I just know
that when we each tell others
our life stories,
about the turning point of our lives,
no matter where we are,
we will have to
acknowledge each other.

Perhaps the telling evokes
a deep, deep feeling inside,
but it is you and I
that have become inseparable
because of this.

And maybe
when the sun has gone down in our lives,
and the end is near;
we can look back at right now,
and know that we have touched
some magical love.

And this is why
I love you.

Because I believe
that such a miraculous temerity,
such profound change,
occurs once in a lifetime.

I do not know what this all means,
Except that we are known
by each other,

And for today,
that is enough.

FACE YOUR DARKNESS!

"Face your darkness!"
you cried out to me.
I cowered in shock at such a notion.
"Tell me of your demons",
you insisted with such fierceness.
But I recoiled at such a possibility.
You stood in front of the classroom,
And I was your only student.

My appearance
was grown up and confident,
even arrogant and angry with you.
You were not supposed to know me
without my consent.
Yet, had you asked my permission
I could never have let you through
my first set of armor.

Boldly, you did not care to ask.
Nothing dampened your feminine tenacity,
and I was wholly unprepared.

"How did you know?"
I begged you for answers,
but you were gone,
and I watched in desperate sadness
as the door closed behind you.

I wanted to give chase,
but I knew that was not my path.
I listened to hear what was already said,

And to grasp a lesson
deeply penetrating.

Now I stand in solitude,
alone in the classroom, with no teacher,
and only echoes of your cries
demanding that I speak of the truth.

You have awakened Love
that arises from the depths:
deep and penetrating Universal Love,
healing and exhilarating.
Not for just one lover.
Not just for you.
Although,
I had already traded in my heart
for a token of your breath,
and
for Life itself.

You, my darling Teacher,
have awakened me
out of the depths of my ancient sleep.
But before leaving,
you opened the hidden floor-board
leading to my own darkness,
that it may shine in the Light,
and finally be truly loved.

Yet by then, you were already gone.

YOUR BEAUTIFUL GAZE HAUNTS ME

This is my place of solitude and comfort,
where the roar of the ocean envelopes me.
I gaze into the beautiful purple waters,
and am reminded of that day when we were here.
I made you my exotic Queen,
and placed upon your head
a circle of purple flowers.
I gently kissed your forehead,
and promised to make you mine.

You remember, my love,
when you secretly knew
That you would come find me...
That I would melt at your first hello,
and I would dive into the depths of your waters,
at our first sweet kiss?

That we would both run
in opposite directions
from each other,
and secretly wish our fingers
were interlocked
for all eternity?

Tell me, my beloved, how does this story end?

THE SPACE BESIDE ME

This is my space
where I wait for you.
No one can take your spot.

I wait for you to sit beside me,
and tell me that your soul
has ended
her long and painful aching
for her true companion.
That your soul has found that in me,
and you will not let this go.

Will you sit beside me?

16

NO LONGER SEEKING

I am no longer seeking to
"rise above" and "transcend".
I am seeking to
delve deep into my unconscious,
to face and examine every dark corner,
to the deepest, darkest depths
of my being.

I long-thought my Ego
was something "bad",
to be fixed and disciplined,
broken and overpowered.

My Ego
has been my
relentless protector,
greatest spiritual motivator, and opponent,
all at once.

I went much deeper,
and taught myself
how to whisper to my Ego
words of calm reassurance,
love for her darkness,
and empowerment
for what is weak and alive
inside me.

That is the only way
to truly accept all of me:
the Shadows, Ego, and the Light;

all are my faithful Teachers,
and depend upon my attendance.

They teach me
both to love and let go
all at once!
as impossible and painful as this all is-
And one day,
Ego gently nudged me
toward a different path.

One that it is lined with
glistening rose-colored diamonds,
One I never could
have seen on my own.

This is the "how" of my Transformation –

The "why" is because
I tripped over you.

I FOLLOWED YOU IN SILENCE

You sought first, and found me
all alone by this tree.
You softly whispered my name,
and I slowly got up to greet you.

You told me your story,
of your heartache, dreams and suffering.
I did not tell you mine.
You beckoned me
with your beautiful eyes and playful smile,
and I jumped right into your center.

I took my time
observing your mind's inner crevices,
And I made your psyche my playground.

I laughed, danced, sang,
cried, told you stories,
read you my poems,
and laid my Love all over you.

I blessed your broken soul,
kissed your cuts and bruises,
and planted flowers where it was desolate.
I breathed life
into your cold, dark cave,
and wrote my name across your walls.
I lit a fire and held you close.

In me
You sought and found

the Great Mother Love that lives inside me.
I sang songs of ancient lovers
whose ghosts still haunt this seaside.

Far surpassing any other human being,
I saw far, far deeper
into your beautiful, ancient, royal soul.
I fell in-love with you,
because the harp songs you played,
so softly melted icy layers
around my sadness.
I simply followed you
in silence and solitude,
trusting the Great Mother Love
that I too saw in you.

Mesmerized by your softness,
your masks,
your hidden treasure chest of buried secrets,
your cuts and bruises,
and the brilliant magician
you play so well –
I patiently waited.

Out of the deep wild inside me,
I pushed you away,
and I find myself forever changed
because you danced to my footsteps.

WHY I WRITE YOU

My Beloved:
Open my letters,
and I will tell you of things
I cannot speak in person.
I seek you every morning
among the Japanese cherry trees,
and I wipe my tears with the leaves that fall.
I feel you next to me,
and I wonder if you seek me too,
from your hiding place.

But what if
you were truly present for me?
Where would our Love go?
Would we run from each other again?
Would we try to mask our fears of each other?

Or, would we embrace with the fierce passion
of a Mother Tiger
for her vulnerable offspring?
Could we pretend
that our hurting each other
never existed?

We will speak, and when we do,
will we hear it in each other's voice:
a thousand cried
and uncried tears of longing?
I love you fiercely,
and if I must, I will wait for you
until we journey back home.

This is why I write you these letters.
They are sent to comfort you,
as you must continue on your wild run
in the dark, mystical forest.
And they allow us the
time, space, and choice to bury
the tragedy of a love
we almost gave birth to.

My Beloved:
will you hold on to these letters,
and if you never come back to me,
will you gently blow them into the wind,
and let Great Spirit return them
to their final resting place?

The birthplace of what felt like the
greatest love ever known.
The story of you and me:

Can you tell them of it in my absence?

THE CENTER OF MY PAIN

I have touched
the center of my pain,
and in discovering
my deep sadness;
I found that in our humanity,
Love's infinite energy,
is pure magic.

I have found strength, courage,
and even my own heart,
as soon as I decided
to stop running from Love.

The rest just happened
and like an alchemist,
I discovered gold
in the simplest aspects
of what has been there all along:

Loving good earth-angels
like you and me.

NO LONGER MY SECRET HIDING PLACE

This is where you came to find me,
my Love.
Remember when I lived here all alone,
for eternity,
thinking I was destined
to be a Slave to my Isolation?

You arrived out of nowhere,
perhaps a response to the
secret and desperate roar
of my Soul.

I kept my terrible loneliness
a forbidden secret.
And there you were
with your gentleness, curiosity,
and tenacious demand for my freedom;
you peered inside my hiding place.

To survive, I became a "Rescuer",
an illusion and projection
of my inherent sense of unlikableness.
Who gave you the right
to expose all of this?!
To breathe in my direction,
and melt my Ice Cave completely away?

You knew if you asked my consent,
I would have never given it to you.
I thought I had to earn your Love
by rescuing you.

Instead, you reached into
my lonely ice cave and touched me
in a way that can never allow
for such an existence again.

You aren't standing here anymore,
and instead of building another ice cave,
I have grown beautiful flowers
as a reminder
of how your presence melted the only home
I ever knew.

It was time to leave this home,
and you were sent from Great Mother Love.
You were so faithful to your purpose,
and my heart will forever write you
poems of love,
tenderness,
and quiet passion.

Thank you, Sweet Stranger,
for you have indeed rescued me.

Will you think of me
when you gaze upon a beautiful flower,
and think of the freedom
in which we will always be bonded?

OUR HOME INSIDE OF ME

This is the beautiful home
inside of me,
where I sit and write for you.
I saw you once,
and so stubbornly fell in-love
with the way your eyes danced
when you looked at me.

I came up with every beautiful story
as I sat here all alone
writing about you.

I told myself that
you were designed in God's perfect image,
and that I was terribly lucky
to have been adored by you.

I told myself of the
infinite possibilities between us,
and that you would love me,
with a deep and penetrating love
that would last for
as long as the sun rises and sets.

I told myself that
it was the working of
Twin Flames
that we finally met.
I ignored the warning signs
that you were elsewhere,
and I stubbornly held on

to my projection of you.

I continued to tell myself
how much your heart weighed
with passionate yearnings for me,
and ignored your silent withdrawal
into your inner whirlpool
of torment, sad confusion
and lonely fear.

I bolted out
On a desperate search
to find your lost, wounded soul
and bring her back to us.

But you had already fled,
running swiftly and fearfully.
The echoes of my crying out
for you
only bounced back.

Laden by guilt,
driven by your silence, and burning
with fierce determination,
I returned here,
and continue to write for you.

Each night, I return
to the spot on the beach
where we connected to each other,
and knew that no goodbye
would ever be final.

Come look for me, my Love,
in this empty house
where I sit all alone
writing about how our Love
once beaconed the seagulls
to surround us.

Come by the beach,
and gather seashells with me,
as the children run ahead.

Hold my face in
your beautiful hands and
lock eyes with me.

Know that this hello is
just the beginning
of building a home
inside of us.

<u>*YOU ARE MY FAVORITE CHANNEL*</u>

My sweet beloved,
I finally stopped crying for you today.
Out of the depths of my grief
emerged a beautiful angel,
who sang me a mystical song, telling
how we are all "channels "
for each other,
and you were one such angel
for me.

I listened intently,
and revealed to her
that my deepest fear was that there was
"just this one person ", and I saw no end
to the depth of my terror.

Such a tragic fear ruled me
into a kept isolation: a death-paralyzing fear
gripping an infant whose caregiver
has only emptiness to return for the baby's
trusting,
needy,
and
love-drenched
gaze.

Through my incredible pain
and subsequent creativity,
I learned that when the channel
has faithfully delivered the message,
it might leave;

not out of rejection,
but out of an unknown
loyalty and fidelity
to other missions.

Perhaps another channel
is already waiting.

Yet here you are with me now,
singing your beautiful songs
of ancient, mystical Love and intimacy,

And once again,
I delight in your presence.

MY PROMISE TO YOU:
A LETTER TO MY CREATIVE ENERGY

I met you long, long ago.
We were on a distant and dark battlefield,
you and I.
I was an infant, and
we fell in-love upon first sight.
I was small and helpless, and
I began to absorb
the toxic, sickening energy of
The Battlefield.

I grew into a weary soldier:
frozen, diligent,
fearful and hidden.
But no darkness
could touch me
as long as you were around.

We wrote beautiful poems together,
we held hands,
and explored the most enchanted places.

In those moments,
and later when I thought of you,
my peace was pure and profound.

Then I got older, and life happened.
I forgot all about you.
I did not want you.
I was ashamed of you, and
you had no more value to me.

I had survived and left
that toxic battlefield.
I believed no one
could touch me.

Recently,
I started writing, creating and
sharing my poems with others.
And to my delight,
that old feeling of our Love returned –
just like old times.

I had forgotten just how lonely I have been for you.
It appears that you, too,
were so desperately lonely without me.

Let us return to our enchanted places,
and I promise you that nothing
will ever come between us again.

YOU ARE MY TRUE LOVE

I woke up last night,
as I was falling asleep.
My fears of loneliness
kept me away from you.
These fears haunt me late at night
after Mother Earth has put Her Children to bed.
I felt that I was waking up from a death:
A death of separation from you.

I am mesmerized by your warm, enveloping Love,
as you have been the most honest
and fulfilling love affair.
You are my True Provider,
yet I sometimes feel
so painfully
disconnected from you.

When I write to you,
it is as a result of
having delved deep into my psyche,
from a place of dancing and swirling
with ancient muses, mystical figures,
and lonely poets.

Lions sit beside me
and encourage me to be brave.

The gorgeous Phoenix whispers
her secrets of strength and resiliency.

The rabbit cautions me to

slow down and observe.

The tigers sit in a circle around me,
and chant memories
of my agile and courageous triumphs.

I am mesmerized by all of this magic,
and I listen to them all.

But there is one magical figure
that holds my gaze most deeply:
The Purple Wizard.

He stares at me intently,
and after a brief moment,
he is gone.

In his place he left me a note.
I try desperately to reach for it,
but I cannot because
I start to awaken from my slumber.

The note has slipped away,
and I caught a glimpse of it.

I think it had your name on it.

YOU CLOAKED ME IN YOUR GENTLE FIRE

I remember
that very cold and dark December night…
I was wandering aimlessly
through the halls of The Mysterious One.
I was a lost and burning Sun,
with no one and nowhere
to shine my Light upon.

I had believed that my Light
would be blown out permanently,
so I sought a Twin Light.
I heard a humming of my name,
and eager for contact,
I immediately sought the source.

There you were,
sitting on a soft blanket of sun,
gently singing a tune,
so strangely familiar.

You called yourself "The Stranger"
and would giggle,
unable to stop the white fire
that danced with you.

Your outstretched arms glowed
with stunning ambers
of gold, blue, and purple.

I took your hand,
and waited for your price –

for your demands of me.
You requested nothing,
except to hum to me
a Melody of Love.

You told me that
a mysterious white light
would heal all my tears and cuts,
smooth over my bruises,
and that you would always
come be with me when I called.

I call for you
once and again, and
each time my tired soul
is rejuvenated when I hear your humming.

I, too, have learned how to hum.
You taught me that this Light flows
from everywhere,
and it is my inheritance.

You told me that I am reborn
into a new moment whenever
I cloak myself in this light.

I am especially transformed
when the wounds begin
to tear at me again.

I love you my Teacher of the Fire.

I hope you know
that when yours runs dim,
I will wrap you in mine, and
you will be pleased by my gentle hum...

the song you often sang to put me to sleep.

MY LONELY SHADOWS

This is my secret stomping ground.
Come find me here, unless
you fear your own darkness
and shadows.
But once you face them,
you might truly be free.
This is what a soulful lonely artist once
whispered in my ear.

So I have been freed, and wait for her
each midnight on Virginia Beach,
where she kisses me with
her words of caution
not to let My Shadows
call me their own.

MY MESSAGE IN A BOTTLE

I wrote the message in that bottle.
I said it does not matter
whether you loved me back.

It does matter if I say
I was hurt or injured by you in some way,
and you extended yourself
to make an amends.

That was the "love" I was seeking.
The rest can be the fantasies created by
genius inventors
of all that is magical to the Heart.

SHADOWS FROM YOUR FIRE

I have mourned with the unresolved pain
of our relationship ending.
I thought it was you
that I was fighting with.

The all-powerful you
that seemingly had such capacity
to reach so deep,
cut so sharp,
and love so gently.

So I went looking for you here.
And I continued begging you
to respond.

Until you emerged
from icy darkness,
the desolate place
I thought was my
final stomping ground.

It was myself I met;
my own voice,
shadows,
and echoes.
It was never you
I was fighting for,
or fighting with.

It was my Demon
made of a dark Fire,

forbidding me
to be seen.

Now I have been seen,
and you have come
crying for me
to come back home.

Never again
will I warm myself
by your black Fire.

True Fire
is already entrenched
in my eager Soul.

LONELY TRAIN-TRACKS:
A MYSTERIOUS AND MAGICAL
UNDERGROUND

She walked alone
along these train tracks,
surrounded by rows and rows of
beautiful colored roses.

She was a small, dark-eyed child,
once held captive
in a maximum-security prison,
located in my unconscious.

She stared at me so intently.
I asked her who she was,
and where she hailed from.
She looked strangely familiar –
a child-like version of me,
but I had never seen her before.

She told me that
she was from my depths,
always kept in a cold and forbidden prison,
alongside many desperate criminals.

I asked her in dismay:
"Who are these desperate criminals,
and what was their crime?"
Her deep brown eyes filled with tears,
but she was too scared to speak.
When she cried,
my chest filled with inexplicable pain,

my stomach felt like she was inside of me,
and had doubled-over crying.

Frightened but curious, I decided to follow her lead.
I did not expect her to put her little hand in mine,
and I could not imagine why she trusted me.
After all, she had been held captive so long,
but it was not me that was holding her captive.
I was determined to find out who was her captor.

We walked for a few miles
along the lonely and dark train-tracks.
Finally, we were standing over a secret trapdoor
beneath a loose track.
It looked like it had been tampered with
numerous times.
The door opened into a well, with a side ladder
covered in rust and cobwebs.
I was frightened and ecstatic at the same time.

The darkness was forbidding, but my yearning for
personal answers burned a deeper resolve.
My small companion timidly reached into her
pocket, and pulled out a small candle and worn out
matchbox.
She seemed to have been here before.
I thanked her for the candle, and once it was lit, we
began our descent.
My heart raced and my head pounded in fear.
I felt her little hand squeeze mine tighter.
She looked up at me with a strangely hollow
sadness, mixed with compassion.
I paused to hug her, but she shook her head.

She had been imprisoned and unloved
for far too long, my gesture foreign and
frightening.

We continued our descent.
She was so much braver than I,
with a gentle resiliency about her.
She was not tough or bitter,
although she recounted how the other prisoners
often taunted her.
They wanted her to be like them, instilled with fear
of the Moss-Monsters leading them
to the secret prison.
They needed to trust no one.
She had almost believed them.

Instead, she knew that she was deeply tired,
hungry for my love,
and oh so lonely.
She did not ask much,
and was grateful for my presence and curiosity.
I could sense her fear about trusting me,
but intuitively, she did.

After what seemed an eternity of
downward decent, we arrived at the bottom.
A cold steel structure awaited us, with no windows,
and surrounded by barbed wire.
The front doors were huge and of ancient iron.
I called out for the Warden.
My heart sounded like roaring ocean waves.
Slowly, a tall, forbidding man emerged.
He was dressed in thick armor,

covered in weaponry,
and had a long beard with silver streaks.
He stared intently at me with his steely grey eyes.
I was unwelcome here,
and he beckoned for the little escapee
to return through the front doors.
She clung fearfully behind me
and began to whimper.
I told her that she was completely safe,
and that I was protecting her.

I whispered to her that she is never going to return
to this prison, under this man's care.
I was determined to keep this promise at all costs!

The Warden was willing to answer my questions
and show me around.
He revealed something strange;
that he has been around for centuries,
and his job was to protect gifted children from the
Moss-Monster.

I was perplexed. How did this concern me?
I did not see myself as gifted;
I never met any Moss-Monsters, and
am I young enough?

He told me a sad tale of a highly sensitive child
being born in a wild and dark forest.
This child was raised by Moss-Monsters
who were cruel, frightening, deceitful, angry,
narcissistic, selfish, and sadistic.
The forest was always dark, damp,

and without any other children.
This particular child had to be protected at all
costs, and so he came to rescue her,
immediately whisking her off to this prison.
In her place, Warden left a Costume
looking identical to her.
Moss-Monsters did not know or care
who was beneath this Costume:
only that she was under their fierce control.

Throughout her life, whenever she had a feeling,
need, or desire,
they were brandished as prisoners,
and immediately sent away,
in the silence of the night,
to this penitentiary.

But these criminals had a secret
in which they delighted:
they have escaped numerous times,
while going undetected for a lifetime.

They posed as other people, relationships,
circumstances,
and intense, raw emotion:
All wearing different costumes.
They had to disguise themselves,
because they knew that they were
considered to be "dangerous".

Warden explained to me that
they were unacceptable to the
hideous and cruel Moss-Monsters,

and to survive, they had to hide or die.
At this point, I was both
mesmerized and riddled with anxiety.
Weren't my original emotions pure and real
and my own?
Was I wearing a costume right now?

I paused to take all of this in.
The Warden's eyes seemed to soften, as I struggled
to understand the meaning of all of this.
I was overwhelmed at how
I was just like everybody else.
We live in a world that promises us
infinite ways of deceiving ourselves.
So we can seemingly go forward and yet remain
the Forever- Warden.
We think we are "happy" and "free because
we got over it", and
"it is in the past".

But these dangerous inhabitants
have a way about them.
They wear the cloak of raw, awkward, intense,
impulsive rage, sadness, narcissism,
feelings of dependency, and
a chronic sense of inferiority.
They take on different costumes...often possessed by
a brooding, violent energy,
because we refuse to understand
how they got that way;
what is the origin of their original pain?

Which burdens have shaped them, fueled them, and

continues to keep them in a desperate circle of
Escape and Return to prison?

Perhaps a loss of love
and a pervasive sense of failure
was the origin of these costumed-characters.
Perhaps this narcissistic scar
is the cloak and dagger
concealing a sense of inferiority
and a lonely desperation.

This morning you may dawn the costume of:
"Perfectionist",
or "Aggressor",
or perhaps none of these are familiar to you.
A mysterious illness may present itself to you,
and call itself the main actor on your stage.

Warden will create and send you
numerous ways to prevent you
from lovingly inquiring into these prisoners.

The next time you are faced with
a painfully familiar situation,
ask yourself:
am I face to face with an escaped "prisoner"?

Light a candle,
and descend into the depths of
your unconscious.
Perhaps there is a small child stuck
in the back wards of the prison
that is too scared to call your name.

Go in search
of this small child.
Call it by your childhood name,
and do not stop
until you hear a faint cry replying to you.

You may feel this child in your chest,
and floodgates of tears
may remove the prison gates off its hinges.

You may not have any access to this prison,
as much as you want to liberate its prisoners.

Perhaps a small, worn out candle
kept somewhere in your unconscious,
may be enough to light the steps
leading down into the well.

Perhaps if you ever arrive there,
your passion, desperation,
yearnings, and centuries of pent up pain,
will melt the prison away.

Cry, cry away and if you should
find this small child, pay attention
to the look in his/her eyes.

If you can, feel the small hand
timidly slip into yours,
and you are on your way.

After all, you may have encountered
the greatest and deepest Love of all.

The power of that Love
may melt away the prison walls,
Warden will soften into a friendly Wizard,
and your prisoners will finally
be free to tell their stories.

Perhaps their stories contain enlightenment
and offer transformation for our Planet Earth.

Would that be worth the risk?

FORBIDDEN CONTENTS

You hide from me
what you are terrified to face in yourself.
Your eyes blaze with fear
as you dare me not to come too close.

Sometimes you stab the box from both ends
using ancient daggers,
releasing your rage and frustration
to bleed all around you.
Many lovers have witnessed you bloody and angry,
and you cared nothing
for their bewilderment.
Your anger and hurt
was a long-forsaken blackness in the setting sun,
and I was mesmerized
by your dark, hypnotic love and rage.

We were both warriors,
fighting invisible demons
that had no identity.

Our battle with one another
was a fierce combination
of running, and then returning
with curious tenderness, and mutual desire
for penetrating intimacy.

Yet, nothing ever softened the terror in your eyes,
until today.
At sunset, in a flash of inspiration
and determination,

I jumped upon your box, and sat on it,
pulling you close to me.
I put my arms around you,
lay my head on your chest,
and wordlessly promised you
that I did not care what was in it, and that
I loved you no matter what might be
your desperate shame.

For the first time I saw you shed
large, sad tears, when you stroked my hair.
Right then I knew that I was permanently free.
I had found
unconditional love
for the first time.

I know what you keep fiercely hidden in your
Forbidden Cardboard Box.
You wanted me to figure it out,
in the hopes that perhaps
I could be the one to set you free.

But you are still running,
and I sit here waiting for you
with arms outstretched,
dancing in the light,
and humming ancient love songs to you.

Sometimes, when the wolves cry at night,
I hear you humming back at me.

My tears and smiles could melt
a thousand stone hearts.

TOO FAST TO BE REAL

My heart is cloaked
and dripping in tears
as I sit alone on the mountaintop.

You are the first
to have stirred the deepest of my emotions.
You awakened my fear of loving someone:
that my heart will be pierced
with six daggers.
Even so, you were too fast to be real.

All of my ideals,
all of my dreams I project upon you
with endless worship.
You were too fast to be real.

My powerful visions of you
follow me wherever I go.

You are the love of my life,
my Inner Muse,
the sweet, delicate wizard holding
an enormous key to my unconscious.

And I cannot know how you came
to possess this power,
because this is your secret
and you guard it
with utmost dedication.

The stunning voice of your soul

captured my own song,
and together, we unlocked
my poetic gifts.
These gifts, along with
thousands of our unshed tears,
have pierced and cleansed
the seven layers of our Souls.

You have inspired me
as if a thousand angels were singing in my ears,
reading me their poems,
and playing on their harps.

Have I fallen
deeply and hopelessly in love with you?
Or do I give up on my canopy of dreams
that I laced all over you?

Is this too fast to be real,
or are you trying to get to me?

Say something,
or the cries roaring from the depths of my
aching, bleeding heart
will awaken ancient dead poets.

Together, we will surround your
silenced, hurt heart,
and awaken Her Voice.

I have truly fallen…

WHO CRIES INSIDE OF ME FOR YOU?

I was once one with my Twin- Flame,
originally born of the same Light.
Of our souls, we were created
from One Love.
You and I were once the same Being;
I was you
and
you were I.
We knew of no separation,
and we delighted
in our true love.

Then came that fateful day
when we were called in for a meeting
with the Great Parent.
We were told that it was time for us
to separate and become two individual souls,
to inhabit two separate human bodies.
We beseeched Great Parent to stop this plan,
and we ached with a pain
that is still felt today.

Great Parent gently wiped our tears,
and promised us a reunion:
that in each of our lifetimes
we will seek and find one another.
We knew this was Great Parent's
unbreakable promise,
and we trusted.

In unspeakable agony,

we faced each other,
slowly closed our eyes,
placed our hands on each other's hearts,
and kissed farewell.

Our ache of separation
reached the heights of the heavens,
across every corner of the galaxies,
and throughout the entire existence
of everything spiritual and physical.

I hear that the angels still cry
when reminiscing about this scene.

I had forgotten about this Great Love
and Great Parent's promise to us,
until very recently when
you came looking for me.

At our first hello, I remembered you.
So it is you that she cries for;
that wise, divine soul of mine
who knows and remembers everything.

I have tried so hard to comfort her,
to convince her that you're unavailable,
and that she will be very hurt if she loves you.

All of these arguments
that have continued to keep me
so terribly lonely in my life –
no longer convince.

She chants stories of how she used to
dance with you,
in the celestial ballroom,
in-love as the cords of light
connected us in a way
no human can fathom.

I am living that ancient pain I felt
at our last goodbye deeply,
although I only encountered you briefly.

All I have is my quill and parchment,
the constant tears that flow from my eyes,
and a soul inside of me whose grief
has completely overtaken me.
I engrave your name in everything I write.

I do not have a mailing address for you -
only a patient and compassionate Universe
who invited me to share my writings with Her.

She reminds me often that Great Parent
hasn't forgotten us,
and in the right time,
will continue to unfold
our first promise.

The promise
has already begun to unfold.

When I feel and hear your voice,
my whole being fills

with inexplicable joy.

I will always worship you
from here on earth,
and when I ever feel
downtrodden and bereft,
I am comforted by what
our heartbeats felt like
at our first good-bye.

YOUR NAME ACROSS A LONELY DESERT SKY

I wandered
across a lonely desert
this evening,
carrying all of my worries and troubles
in the little sack
that hung from the edge
of my walking cane.

I had first journeyed
through beautiful green pastures,
and at the edge,
I wandered into the lonely desert.

I do not know why I was led there,
or who was guiding my steps.

The desert beckoned me as fiercely
as the wind that blew all around me.
There was little life here,
but a profound sense of mystery,
and a haunting echo.
I cautiously stepped forward,
and took in the mystical surroundings.

I begged the question:
how can such a desolate and lonely desert
have a wind so powerful, whispering Her secrets
through my clothes?
I could hear her,
I could feel her,
but I could not see her.

"Tell me", I cried out, *"of what are you made?*
Why do you choose to speak to me?!"

She gently laughed, and told me that
she knew I always see her name,
and my heart flutters.

I confessed to her my longings
for her secrets,
her gentle whispers,
and my readiness
for her embrace.
Wind howled all around me,
and she instructed me
to close my eyes.
When I did, I felt a gentle tug at my legs,
and her whispers got louder.

A hot wind enclosed my entire body,
and the deepest sense of safety
enveloped within.

I turned to walk away,
but in front of me was a pit
I had not seen before.

Was it was magically placed there?
A brief terror
struck a chord through my body.

She instantly sensed my fear:
"If you are not misguided you will not fall",
she softly shouted to me.

I looked back for the last time,
and beamed my smile
of gratitude and love.

With the warmest wind,
she envelops me
in a cloak of maternal, unconditional love.

In the desert, she speaks to me
words of wisdom and grace...
and every time I see her name,
my heart flutters.

CHILDREN OF MY SOUL: A PROMISE KEPT

I remember an ancient meeting
we had long ago.
You with the Great Parents
spoke with my Twin-Flame and I,
informing us that
it was time to separate.

They said that it would be painful,
but they would gift me with
the yearning to write; that
parchment, ink and words
would be a part of your light
inside of me.

You asked me to tell you
of my journeys,
to write home as often as I needed to,
and share my letters
with Humanity.

Sitting by my writing table
I gaze into the fireplace,
and cry to you,
speaking of the realities
of human existence.

Sometimes I cry so intensely
that my tears
blind the words on my pages.

My fallen tears,
the ink and blurred words –
they all hold each other,
and their sobs are heard
throughout the forest.

With my hands, I send you
the songs of my heart, some of which are dipped
in the most profound human emotions.

Some of my letters to you
are comprised of words that are dancing
to the tune that humans cannot hear;
it is for the angels only.

But these writings of mine,
they are my promise back to you:
that I will always communicate with you
until the day
we are once again reunited.

I trust that you will take my words
and cradle them
in your arms.
And when you do,
stroke them, love them, and sing to them,
like a mother caresses
her beloved child.

For these words of mine...
they are the Children of my Soul.

They are my gift to you, and I deliver them
to your care
with utmost trust
in your guardianship.

I call upon you, my Good Parent,
to see the vulnerability in these children...
their need for your protection,
their profound joy
at having been brought to life
by one of your own,
who never betrays a promise.

THE UNLOCKED MAGIC OF THE LONELY WANDERER

I am the Lonely Wanderer.
I have travelled throughout the planet,
and across the seven seas.
I have climbed through mountains,
caved in jungles,
and lived among the wild.

I joined the circle of animals, plants and fish,
and we loved and embraced each other.

From people I stayed away,
always feeling distant and apart.
But these fish, plants, animals and nature:
they were my home.
In their presence
I found consolation
and the meaning for my existence.

I never questioned my fate or purpose;
their love was completely unconditional.
Forty years went by, and one day
I stumbled upon an ancient and cold bonfire.

There was magnetic energy
drawing me in.
This was the meeting place of lovers and poets...
considered sacred ground.

Ancient mythology says that no one leaves here
without some secret door

inside of them unlocking,
never to be closed again.
I heard of this place, but was frightened
of its potential power over me.

Now, this place visited me.
I was fascinated and terrified,
for I never had any such experiences
about 'love', '
secret doors unlocking' or '
an encounter with lovers and their poets'.

I only heard about it
through the whispers of the humans
in the nearby villages.
I listened closely
and I felt the roar of tears, goodbyes, new hellos,
and their ongoing conversations
speaking of hope, romance,
desperate love,
and undying passions.

Suddenly, flames surrounded it,
and you appeared before me.
I was shaken and terrified;
"Who called you to my existence?!"
I desperately shouted,
trying to send my anger before me
to conceal the piercing vulnerability
that began to consume me.

But you just smiled and giggled;
we were together again

and that is all that mattered.
You were scared, but your strong, gentle soul knew
it was time for us to meet again.

I faced you
despite all my efforts
to hold back a damn of tears.

"What about separation, abandonment, and fear
of being hurt?"
My voice shook
as I tried to hide the pain
of all the lonely suffering
of those who wandered here.

My desperation and panic
were mounting by the second.

Then suddenly they came alive...
all the ancient lovers and poets
that once knew the magic of this bonfire.
They held hands and circled us,
and when I had the courage to open my eyes,
there you were in the center.

Your eyes brimmed with tears,
as you struggled to maintain your composure.
"Follow me Lonely Wanderer",
you gently whispered:
"I promise to always know you...
Now your magic has been unlocked,
and you are free."

And all at once,
you were gone, fading into the mist, to join
the lovers and their poets.

I cry for you every single day,
and I call your name always.
And I hear you echo me back everywhere that I go,
and in every moment that I am.

I am closer to people now.
I share the magic you have unlocked in me.
And should you return to this bonfire
close your eyes and listen closely:
you will hear me encouraging you to be brave,
and face your fear of losing me.
Love never leaves –
it only changes form.

This you have taught me,
and this is part of the magic
you have unlocked for us all.

CONVERSATIONS BETWEEN OUR SOULS

Long at last we meet again,
hailing from yonder
and seeking each other's company.
We have both traveled far
and are exhausted from our journey.

Our souls committed
to meet at this particular time and place,
in faithfulness to an old promise long before
we were dominated by our human egos.
Without knowing our true names,
we knew something powerful,
deep, profound, and endlessly aching,
existed for each other.

Next to this ancient echo,
we met face to face with a war
between our egos.

Our terrified hearts took flight,
but our beautiful souls never stopped
conversing with each other.
They are old friends,
and are not going to let our egos interfere
with their delightful exchange
of secrets.

You showed me the room in your house
dedicated for me,
so this Lonely Painter
can sit and paint with her voice

all the days of her life.

You offered me this
beautiful writer's den,
so my thirsty soul can pour out
her yearnings and songs
for you.

You put down the beautiful vase of flowers
with fierce determination, and turned to
leave the room.
Will I be able to take it in
that you have brought me home?

Why must you leave so soon?
Take me to the closet
where your demons hide,
and allow me to know
if I can go to sea with them.

I will take the old, black steam train to you
and remind you of our promise
that this conversation
is forever.

THE DAY I REMEMBERED YOU

When I first looked into your eyes,
I urgently began my search
for the Universal secret
of Love.

With courage, heartache, curiosity and
a lifetime of lonely pain,
I climbed into a sturdy old wooden ship,
and set sail for my journey
throughout the Universe.

I started out on the Ocean
and introduced myself to her.
I said that I was the Lonely Wounded Poet,
and I was seeking her answers
to Love.
She softly said
that in order to find answers,
I would have to courageously dive
deep to her depths, and there
I would find myself.

I then ran with the Wind,
asking him
what were his secrets of love?

He said
that I would understand love
when I ran free and wild,
and knew what that felt like.

My next meeting was on the Beach.
I humbly kneeled on her soft surface,
and felt her butterfly kisses
on my face.

She told me that I would need to
lie down in softness,
take time to inhale, and welcome
tranquility.

I then went into the Forest,
calling out my questions of Love.
He called out that
I would need to release
the fear of my own strength,
and not run from
love anymore.

My journey
was drawing to a close,
and my final visit was to the
most remote village in the world.

It was almost desolate,
but for a few old people
rumored to be descendants
from settlers many centuries ago.

I asked them their secret of love,
and they replied
that it is found in the words
of a thousand roses.

One old woman took my hand
and gently put it
on her face.
I could feel her warm tears
as they journeyed down the map
of thousands of years.

She held it there for some time, and
the only sound
was of our heartbeats.

She held my gaze and said:

"Love is an agreement and
conversation between two souls.
The conversation began
when your soul was first split in half,
and you thought your pain
would never end.
Keep still
whenever you desire to slam the door,
and to run far away.
Keep still
when you deny its existence,
or make demands of it.

Care for your soul
like the ocean waves that dance across your chest,
the wind that runs wild and free with you,
the sandy beach that wraps you in her arms,
and the strong trees
that surround and empower you.

For this love
is from another dimension,
a sacred energy
that has once again
kept her promise to you.

The promise to come find you,
free you,
and complete
both of you."

And when I opened my eyes,
they were gone.

In their chair
they left me
a note
reminding me
that all this time
we had never let go of each other's hand.

And I sat down and wept...

TELEPATHIC ENTANGLEMENT: BONDS THAT HAUNT AND HEAL ME

Long and sweeping deserts called my name,
and I wandered for centuries.

The profound silent desert
claimed me as his,
although the wind cautioned me
not to get too comfortable.

In this desolate plane
I relished the tension of loneliness,
and the softest tenderness for Love
that eluded me.

One day I saw a single page
swirling in front of me,
going around and round,
dancing happy circles around me.
I kept walking but this paper followed me,
persistent with his mission.

The Wind whispered to pick it up and read it.
I ignored his voice,
although the Wind
has been such a loyal friend.

The Sand, she beckoned me to lift it up,
blowing secrets and possibilities
in my direction.

But my stubborn ego refused

the possibility of vulnerability.

Although weary and hurting from loneliness,
I kept my fierce march of avoidance,
like a loyal soldier protecting
an orphaned infant.

Without notice,
these pages began multiplying,
swirling all around me.

I was helpless and angry,
and my rage started a fire.
The pages quickly began to burn.

To my dismay,
the words turned into a
beautiful song.
Letters lifted from the pages and
each was its own flame.

They called my name,
and told me that my time
of lonely wandering
has come to an end.

That no matter what I did,
or how hard
I ignored these sacred words,
Love has come to rescue me.

I turned to the dancing letters,
and having lost myself

in the joyful possibility,
took their hands and we danced
under the beautiful night sky.

The stars formed your name,
and your beautiful light penetrated my body.
I have finally come to terms that
in your arms you carried me,
and within your Flame
I am born again.

From that moment I began to sing
songs of poetry for you,
creating words for the unsayable.

I wrote you poems
that speak about your love
in the shape of a golden, ancient key.
A key that has tenderly opened a lock
distorted and stuck
from centuries of rust.

In our psychic dialogues
I have known myself.

In the unknowingness
we have come
to our final resting place.
And in having come full circle,
after many painful lifetimes,
we return to our place of birth:
One Flame.

Lonely Poet still wanders through
many vast sand deserts,
leaving sheets of paper
where no one looks.

On the paper are written
secrets of love,
whispers of possibility,
and the opportunity to awaken
hungry, lost ghosts
of childhood nurseries.

For these ghosts...
they are powerful.

They have the power
to burn fires of rage,
or lead the wanderer back
to the other half of their Flame.

"Choose wisely",
whispers the Wind...
"Pick up the sheet of paper
and hold it against your cheek"
beckons the Sand.

And across the desert night sky,
I see your name,
forever beckoning me
to write you words
of poetry,
love and possibility.

<u>*YOUR BEAUTIFUL WHITE PICTURE FRAME*</u>

*I sat alone with your photo last night
adorned by a beautiful white picture frame,
the only memory left of you.
I cried out to the God of Love,
in the stillness of the night,
pleading for the permission and courage
to unlock my heart for you.*

*God of Love revealed
that you were sent as the key
to unlock me,
but that only
Time
will decide
when it is time
to open
the sealed gates.*

*I had met you with a long and tired list
of what "love" should be.*

*You were none of these,
and stubbornly refused
to abide by man's rules.*

*You opened doors inside
that can never
be closed.*

*I helplessly witnessed
as you unleashed*

my creativity,
rage,
darkest of emotions,
and most beautiful of songs.

Songs that speak of
sealed gates rattled open
after centuries of
deep slumber and secrecy.

Sleeping shadows have awakened,
and have begun
dialogues with me.
Demons have come forward
and speak their tale
of having been
created and unveiled.

And here I sit,
gazing deep into your beautiful eyes
looking for clues as to where
you are hiding now.

In your eyes,
I have to fight to hold back the river of tears
that are more powerful than anything
I have ever experienced for anyone.

When we last said goodbye,
you thought I was not looking
when you slipped
the other half
of your heart inside of me.

*Ever since then,
I have been carrying around
two heartbeats,
and both
cry for us.*

LOVE IS A DANCE
IN THE CELESTIAL BALLROOM

Midnight has approached,
and we meet in the Celestial Ballroom.
The portal
to this stunningly beautiful ballroom
is your still, silent photograph.
I call you to join me
by blowing through
the dark red and orange flames,
and within moments,
we are crying, laughing and dancing
on the cosmic ballroom floor
where the celestial beings
celebrate our union.

I sent you this letter
to explain where the music is coming from,
as it is unfamiliar to your own heartbeat,
and its sudden intensity
perplexes you.

When you were not looking
that fateful day we said goodbye
in the middle of the deserted fields,
I slipped the other half of my heart inside
of your heart's orchestra.

So when your tears flow like a powerful river,
you hear celestial music playing,
and rivers of deep emotion escape you,
do not be alarmed.

It is only calling you to our dance
in the heavenly ballroom
where celestial beings
await our entry.

There they watch us dance,
and shed tears,
that turn into colorful diamonds of joy
at our perfect freedom
to love one another.

SECRETS IN YOUR EYES

Forbidden tales
you keep guarded from the world.
Running, running to catch
the old, black steam train, ever so desperate
to keep up your chase.

Fear, pain, and uncertainty
have flooded
your tender, sensitive, artistic mind,
and you frantically search
for an escape.

People, they have betrayed your company,
and lost souls have
wrapped themselves
around your feet.

To the world,
you show beautiful eyes,
dancing with vibrant colors,
piercing into the very
hidden corners of their soul.

You are so observant, and you keep this
hidden so they cannot
steal it from you.
Gentle, sensitive,
and so very vulnerable,
you hide behind a beautiful exterior,
playing the role, they threw on you
when you were born.

Catering to their wishes,
fulfilling their demands,
smiling at their beckoning, you run into
the open arms of promising love.
Your hopes get violently dashed, and your heart
shatters in millions of broken, sharp pieces.

You are the Artist,
but hidden
with all of your priestly blessings,
great ability to connect with the Divine,
and magical touch into the hearts of the weak,
you are a trapped prisoner.

You run freely
through the halls of your self-protective dungeon,
forever forbidden
to taste the sweet fruit
of true freedom.

You wrap yourself
in an old worn out shawl at night,
rocking yourself to sleep,
as your sobbing awakens
the sleeping dungeon guards.

You are so beautiful, creative and talented,
and no one knows that you are running,
always looking back, desperate
to escape your demons
that are on an angry hunt for your soul.

You have not told me any of this,

terrified I will judge and leave you,
rejecting your shattered heart
and denying you the love
you so desperately hope for.

You just smile at me,
gazing at me
with those beautiful eyes
that the world has fallen in-love with.

"Do not worry," I gently whisper to you,
"I shall never speak of this tale to anyone".

And then you were gone,
leaving behind one last note to me:

"It is your own prison you have looked into.
These demons... they are your own.
This black train, which haunts you,
is one you have been on for centuries.
I am you, and now you must
follow her lead to come
find me".

Lost and bewildered,
I crumpled up the note, and
frantically searched for you.
It was too late.

Defeated and alone,
I sat on the stone cold floor, wrapped myself
in a worn out shawl, and cried
until the sleeping dungeon guards

carried me home.

You were right there waiting for me.

I collapsed into your arms,
wrapping us both in this worn out shawl,
feeling like innocent babies
for the first time.

AN ANCIENT VISITOR

I did not know where you hailed from,
and why you suddenly appeared
in my secret room.

Without my consent,
you began to search my cardboard boxes.
You stayed busy, while I sat in the corner
and watched: bewildered, and overwhelmed.

First sadness,
and then the heights of joy
overcame me,
and none of my protests
stopped you.

You kept searching fiercely
and tenaciously
rifling through my storage.

No one said you were coming –
I was not expecting you; and at a loss
in knowing how to handle you.

After two months,
you finally stopped searching
and turned around.
You had found something
terribly precious,
and I was not at all aware of it.

It was in a cardboard box,

which had not been opened
in twenty-three years.
You took it with you to the fireplace,
and cautiously opened it.

"But this is my secret property,
and you did not ask me for permission!"
I cried to you.

You gently nodded for me
to sit down next to you.
You took charge, and
I felt a strange trust and peace
in this moment.

I asked you for an explanation,
and you said there were things that
you alone must do.

A sense of forbidding came over me,
as you came close to unpacking
this old cardboard box.

I got strength from your gentle, sweet face,
your reassuring glance,
and peaceful presence.

We both sensed
a monumental moment in our lives,
something fate long-planned,
even before our birth.

I waited with baited breath,

my heart beating louder than
thundering wild horses,
and my mind swirling with black steam trains
racing through it.

You opened the old, musty box'
and there it was:
my first typewriter I had long abandoned.
You gently lifted it placing it on my lap.
"You must pick up where you left off, my love.
The world needs your words,
and you must not hide
your gift from us."

I panicked because I had not used
my faithful typewriter
for so many years.

I had long forgotten
about my love affair with words,
as life got in the way.

Perhaps I had lost my creativity,
my connection with that
deep roar of emotion
that no one can explain.

What if we had become separated –
the words and I?
What if I long-forgot how to
go down into the ocean and
return with jewels

to touch other souls?

I sat alone with her:
a once faithful companion
who helped me put words
into poems of love,
connection, and evoking tales
that have not been told in hundreds of years.

When I looked up,
you were gone, and I knew
you had fulfilled your mission.

If you are looking for me, my ancient love,
come find me
in the room where you left me.

There are now flowers, scented candles,
soft music, and a beautiful white frame
adorning your angelic face.

I sit here and write for you,
but in that turn of events, I have come to fulfill
an old and forgotten dream:
to connect with my universe,
to love many people,
to share with them my soul.

And when they peer into my soul
through these writings,
they will see themselves.

If they look a little deeper,

they may just see
my undying love for you.

If they have eyes that understand hidden messages,
they may glimpse a fierce flame
that returns to me in every lifetime,
and keeps the promises
once whispered by moonlight.

THE WAR BETWEEN
INVISIBLE CHAINS AND THE LIGHT

I came looking for you this morning,
running through vast fields of green,
with rays of light raining down.

This stunning light was from yonder, and
I desperately wanted to share it with you.

I ran wild and free,
up and down the hills,
crying out your name.

I never felt such joy,
such an exhilarating
vibrant pulse of Life,
and I finally understood "God".

Light and Love rained down on me,
and I was entirely free.
But I could not embrace my new freedom,
because I knew you were still trapped and alone.

I ran up and down these hills,
until I heard a silent cry
from a small building on top of the hill.

Like a dutiful soldier
running like a madman to save an orphan,
I ran up the hill
and burst into the room.

There you were,
and to my dismay, the room was empty
with dust, cement and wooden planks everywhere.
This room was cold and neglected,
with no evidence of love
ever having marched through here.

You looked so forlorn,
determined to keep your chains
around your love-object.
Both of you, a prisoner and a prison-guard,
each terrified of the same thing.

What you were holding on to
was nothing resembling spiritual love
which never leaves its footprints in chains.

"So come with me into the sunlight",
I shouted gleefully to you.
But you refused to leave your prisoner.

I pleaded with you:
"I must leave here,
because love never takes prisoners,
never carries chains or ropes,
and instead fills a room
with sweet flowers
and celestial music.
There is none of that here, my love!
Come with me!"

I began to back out, my chest heaving
from uncried rivers of tears,

flowing from my desperate sadness for you.
I hoped you would follow me,
and that you would drop your end of the chains,
so you both can be free.

But you remained,
and my heart has not stopped crying
for us both.

Life has gone on,
and I continue to roam free
in the Fields of Light,
running everywhere
like a free young child.

This is my joyful world,
but incomplete without you.

I still call out your name,
hoping you will join me.

Sometimes I see a fleeting image of you,
feel your warmth next to me,
and hear your soft kisses in my ear.

Other times, you appear to guide me
along my journey,
and let me know that
you never really left me.

I never know if these are projections
born in my mind's powerful capabilities,
or if you temporarily left your prison and

have come to love me again
for a single moment.

I considered visiting you again in prison,
but the thought is too much to bear.

I stand outside sometimes,
and sing your name,
whistling through the window.

I know that you can hear me,
because when I turned and walked away
for the final time,
you came running after me.

Finally, oh finally, we run hand in hand
through the fields of light.

There are no more prisons, prisoners,
or prison guards.
Only two playful children running together
in fields of light, love,
and spiritual romance.

And you knew all along
that I would come back for you,
and at once
when you were ready,
you would follow me home.

YOU THOUGHT YOU COULD
HOLD BACK YOUR LOVE FOR ME

Deep in our unconscious
there was a touch that happened
the first time we met, and we both knew it.

Far enough,
and away from her
there lived The Exile.

Young and terrified, she remained
under the veil,
without a touch or a voice.
Long before you saw her, she blankly stared,
frozen within the prison walls.

Few people knew of her existence,
and never of the infinite well of
intense emotions she carefully guarded.
I did not know of her,
and not even I
could free her.

She did not speak my language,
although I tried everything
to release her silence.

Then you touched me briefly,
and she came forth.
Veil removed,
eyes closed,
beautiful hands

together in a prayer,
radiant light emanated from her hands,
a love so deep
I was startled out of my illusions.

She dedicated a shrine to you inside of me,
comprised of the fierce and pure love
of a wild and holy child.

I asked her what freed her
after lifetimes in Exile.

She answers me night after night
whispering that I was really loved.

It has been so long
since I have seen you,
and yet I still lie awake each night
pondering such a capacity
for intense emotions
that poets have
not yet named.

So I decided to share my love-letters
with the world,
in the hopes that you will come across them,
and know that I too,
could not hold back my love for you.

<u>YOU ARE FOREVER IN MY TEARS</u>

"There is no such thing as good-bye"
I whispered in your ear.
I wipe the tears off your face,
your arms hugging me so tightly,
sobs reverberating
throughout the vast dark seas.
Our ship rocks back and forth,
winds howling all around us.
I cannot stop crying with you,
for the possibility of good-bye
is always haunting us.

My mind plays tricks on me,
telling me that you are just
a figment of my imagination,
when I knew the whole time we can never
say good-bye.

So vulnerable we are both now,
seeing through each other's veil,
knowing that as long as I have a heart,
she will speak stories to you and
write you love-letters.

You are seeking up the ladder,
trying to climb out of your mind's prison,
while I sit so far away
wondering where you are.

This is how I know you are my other half:
a longing that is not from this world,

secret talks between our hearts, and I never tire
of gazing at your picture.

I wipe my tears as they fall from your face,
knowing that once again,
I will turn to the Mother Earth
for her love and comfort.

My prayer for you emanates
from the 7th layer of my soul.
This is the layer that speaks only of
love, God, and the truth.
She cries out for you,
and today I heard her telling me
to write you letters,
because you need them too.

My prayers for you - they escape from me,
and run wild
through the halls of heaven, begging for answers.
They are like wounded, lost
orphan children
in a desperate search for their parents.

This is how I pray for you.
I pray to the Being who brought us together
to bless you, and watch over you.
That wherever you are,
and wherever you go,
whomever you choose to love,
that you are happy,
and if we have to let each other go,
we do so with grace and forgiveness.

This trail of tears I have left behind
speaks of the unspeakable emotion
we have for each other.

This trail of tears leaves an echo behind,
and I hope one day
you will come and visit with me.

Bring with you the ladder that you climb,
for I have sunk deep inside
to a place I have never met.

THE MAGICAL RIVER OF LOVE

Today I remembered our talk
by the River of Light.

It was just the two of us,
enjoying our deep love for each other.

For a moment in time,
we knew of no pain,
suffering, or separation.

Prior to our meeting,
the poems and songs of love, were cast aside
for fools and the brokenhearted.

We laughed at the lonely poets,
thinking they were wasting their time
speaking of such madness
called 'love'.

And now you and I
have created this dense enormously powerful
River of Light,
and across this river are the hands of all
the lovers in the world
reaching for each other.
How much I delight in our creation, my love!
I, too, used to cry over you,
willing to sacrifice my life
just to breathe in your soul.

And now I have you always and forever,

and for this I rejoice!
Today I finally found it:
a river of life, light, love and joy,
and I made you this promise.

I promise to walk next to this river
for all the days of my life.
I promise to dip into this
river of golden light, and produce
beautiful words of love for you,
and for all of humanity.
And when I feel lonely for you,
I will look across it, deep into it,
seeing it right next to me.

I have come to experience
that you surround me,
because we are born of this light.
This deep, thick golden light belongs
to us all.

We are finally free, as we reach
for each other,
sending words of beautiful music,
poems of love,
and depth of touch that
we so yearn for.

Will you meet me here again?

<u>*YOUR HEART IS MY MIRROR*</u>

I thought it was just you - do you remember?
I once believed that I could not love
anybody but you.
I was aching in every corner of my existence,
yearning for your breath upon my soul.

So I continued to travel the globe, lost and forlorn,
never understanding what you tried to teach me.
I had said good-bye to you:
not because I wanted to,
but because the time came
to part and to delve deep
into individual unconsciousness
for answers.

I dove deep, but I did not know
if I could hold onto my faith any longer.
I kept hearing your voice
throughout my veins,
a love-song
that was a constant prayer.

So I kept going, hoping beyond hope
that I would meet you there –
wherever I go.

When I looked deep into their eyes,
I saw your beauty in their beauty,
and I felt comforted.

Along the way,
I stopped to love them,
marveling at how similar you were.

Sometimes the tears would engulf me,
and I would seek a quiet corner in the marketplace
to cry and pray for you.

That is how I know you are close to me:
I feel your love as
rivers of prayer throughout my body.

And I remained traveling on
foot, boat, and camelback
throughout the vast planet earth.

Some of the most beautiful places I have been to,
did not have a name,
without any human investments...

just a wandering of my heart
seeking her place
of surrender.

To kneel down, and let myself
feel for a moment
the pause of a pain
that always seems to escape me
when I think of you coming back home.

Why must I feel this pain
and longing
so deeply?

Putting my hands on your head
and reading words from
the ancient secret book
can ease my longing.

Do you remember
when those words became our shelter,
filling us with love and comfort?

We said, "I love you",
and then parted to travel
in search for meaning
in the hearts of humans,
many who have
mirrors inside of themselves.

I look inside their hearts and see
such a stunning reflection,
an echo of your voice
and such tender,
wise, kind eyes.

Now I can return home,
for I have realized your mission for me.
I now carry my own mirror,
and I never stop waiting for you
to look inside of me.

If this causes you to kneel down and weep,
turn your palms upward
and know your tears to be
our blessing for Mother Love.

You weep, because in me you found
what you are seeking:
your love, your heart,
and your own mirror.

IS THIS OUR LAST GOODBYE?

I came to you this evening, in our exotic land
where all lovers meet
to bequeath their hearts to each other.

I asked you, once again,
if you will accept my invitation to love,
and you remained silent.

And so,
I took our love into my mind's province,
and instructed it
to travel directly to our souls.

Here we are forever free
to roam like wild lovers,
young and crazed with this intoxication
called romance.

Your heart came with mine,
and we soared through the realm
of Divine Feminine Love.

We spoke to each other
in a language our minds cannot understand,
and have encountered myriad delights
within our unconscious.

In this province,
we restored each other
as we unburdened
our Exiles

as witnesses of healing for one another.

We faced our neediness,
gifts, buried creativity,
capacity for love,
and everything
both human and divine in ourselves.

The Exile in me
has been miraculously freed because of us,
and now she is free to live and thrive
in my heart's playground.

Know that my infinite tenderness for you
is beyond the realm of humanity.

It exists forever
in our Exotic Unconscious Playground,
and if you put your ear close to my photograph,
you can hear us laughing,
playing wild and free.

This is where we remember
our young and crazed intoxication
for a love only known by a language
our minds cannot understand.

I can never say our last good-bye.
Can you?

LOOKING FOR MY LOST SPARKS

I heard your voice call to me today,
asking to meet me alone,
in a place of pure paradise.

I was frightened at the notion,
because this deep secret
I keep carefully guarded from the world.

My secret is
losing my place inside when I meet you.

A sacred and intense bonding flame
is ignited for me in loving and being loved.
At such a profound moment, I am led
to the meeting point of my psyche.

I so desperately search for my lost sparks,
and when I am able to look inside a human heart,
I find one of them.

If I linger too long,
I become terrified of the attachment
and the heat of such light
frightens me away.

After all,
I have been a lonely wanderer all my life,
seeking my lost flames.

Once I encounter them,
I am flooded

with the pain of goodbye
and I cannot bear to walk away.

Beyond my control
I fell deeply into your eyes, that day,
when you gazed at me softly.

Something about your voice
brought me a strange comfort,
and in that moment
my soul sparked a fire for you.

This fire has your eyes, kind heart
and dancing dimples,
but my laugh, smile
and gift for words.
She is wise like both of us,
but wild and carefree.
She is not attached to anything,
and yet she loves all that is Life.

I stopped to speak with her the other day,
and I told her about you.
I spoke of my fear of the closeness,
the love, the distance, and my need for both.
She replied that for me to come alive
I would need to stand near you,
and allow the heat from your flame
to warm my lonely heart.

Yea, I fought, pleaded, begged,
and talked my way out,
for the fear of losing love

is more powerful than any answers
the mind can discern.

I started to walk away with finality in my step
and sadness in my little light.
She began to grow dim from the tears I cried inside,
and soon she would be just a lonely wick
with only memories of burning love
and a carefree wild dance.

But suddenly you appeared in front of me:
regal, wise and observing.
This is when you told me
to meet you tonight
in our secret place of pure paradise
infused with love and celestial perfume.

We met at the stroke of midnight,
and I fell into your arms: shyness, fear,
and desperate anguish of my lonely existence
falling away like feathers on a breezy day.

I stayed in your arms,
and fiercely allowed myself this moment
of intense attachment to you,
and with you.

That spark inside me,
once a cold memory,
came to life
and became one with yours.
It was in this one instant that I knew of no threat -
only a joy without bounds

in having the fire inside of me
dance with her tribe.

I do not have to bear to say goodbye to you,
because these two lost sparks know they will live on,
beyond the body form.
They made a pact long ago
to love each other deeply
and for all eternity.
Lifetimes will come and go,
our bodies, names and faces will change,
but never the love between these two flames.

A friendship
and a pact made ancient lifetimes ago;
for love, seeking and finding,
and at each reunion, one spark
that is about to die from lonely grief,
is brought alive by the touch of the other,
who sparks a singing fire inside
that no one else can see.

I STOPPED THE SUN TODAY

My feather dipped in ink,
and the eager blank parchment,
awaiting the music from my typewriter,
guides my fingers.
I write you this
because I had to let you know
how I stopped the sun today.

As my fingers dance on the keyboard
and draw elegant strokes on this piano,
I recount the deep and earnest beseeching I did
when your face appeared before me.
Every once and again I cannot help
stroking your face and kissing your forehead,
and waves of love for you
overcome my lonely soul.

I first fought with your image
and commanded it to leave me,
for the sadness engulfing my being.
But that just filled me with infinite pain,
and I watched tears fall from your eyes.

I decided to try something different,
since this battle of yearning for you
has been too long and arduous.
I slowly began to sing your song...
softly, gently, with love and compassion for you.

I looked above your head
and saw the sun stop,

and the tears dry upon your face.

I did not expect the blood
that runs through my veins to grow so hot,
and I became mesmerized with the sun.

I sang until your face faded away,
my blood called out for Life itself to lie beside her,
and the sun
returned to her movement.

Slowly the sun had set,
and your face simmered
above the ocean surface.
You called out to me,
and it was your turn to sing my song.

You sang me a song of the spirit,
carefree and overtaken by pure joy.
The lyrics told me that I was safe
and that heaven would always be my protector.

I did not cry, nor run
nor question your song for me,
and when your face began to fade
along with the sun going down,
I grabbed your hand,
and we were pulled into the beautiful waters,
to drown in our intoxicating love.

So you sing for me, and I sing for you.
My fingers have found their home on this piano;
creating paintings on a canvas

I call your heart.

I still fight with myself, every now and again,
resisting being rocked
to another dimension by our love.
I still cry and beseech the sun to stop
long enough to turn time back.
But as you are faithful to me,
you return in front of me
when I whistle your name.

Your beautiful gaze
fills me with tender reassurance
that we are meant to swim
in the ocean of the spirit,
and that love will always come back to get me.

I do love you, Oh Beloved One,
have I not told you that already?

YOUR BEAUTIFUL VOICE
HEALED A LONELY HERMIT

I came to the end of my day's journey,
tired and weary
from the torments of their souls.

Each day I walk along the village's edge
and spend time with the lost, the abandoned
and the forlorn.
They tell me of their losses and heartaches,
and I feed them some figs and water
from my leather pouch.
They do not ask for much
but a kind soul to visit with them.

Every morning, at dawn,
I walk along the same cobblestone path
that takes me to the forgotten alleys of my village.
Each night at sunset on my return home
I gaze at an apple tree,
marveling at her beauty.

I do not understand much about life,
except that we who walk this planet
have chosen this existence
and are desperate to seek a meaningful path.

In all my encounters with folks
I ask them one thing:
"tell me on which theater
do your energies most flow?"
I am never sure what answer to anticipate,

and yet their answer is always the same:
"*Love!*" they shout.
I ask them to explain in a more personal way,
and this is their message to me:
"*Love is my true Mother*
from which I exchange the most energy.
When I can relate to another person
in an untrammeled outpouring of limitless love,
I feel most alive and with purpose".

I took their words to heart
and thanked them for their stories.

As I walked home,
I pondered on why we hold back so much
on our innate exuberance
to love each other.

Man searches for pleasure, satisfaction
and avoidance of pain.
But have we plunged the depths
of the need for love?

What happens when this need overpowers us,
and we cannot overcome our inner obstacles?

I wipe away tears
as I cry for all those in my human family
who must wrestle with this dilemma.

A soft rain began to fall
and she kissed the tears on my face.
She gently wrapped me in her arms,

creating a vessel of motherhood around me.

Perhaps love is like a gentle yet fierce rain,
and we need to receive it
with the innocence of an openhearted child.

Perhaps love is an energy that flows
like a confident warrior
marching to his own beat.

Is it also a potent, holy strength
that can leave us with wounds
if we are not cautious?

Does forbidding caution
permeate our inner galaxy,
and hold us back?

"I know of such dilemmas",
I cried under my breath,
"because I am Love's Explorer
forever tracing the source
of her mighty river".

That is when I saw you from across the stream.

You were magnificent
in your royal promise to me,
and all at once,
I knew that it was time
for me to finally sit back
and inhale your song.

YOU NEVER PROMISED
TO LOVE ME BACK

I sat with you on the riverbank,
and gazed at the beautiful sunset,
so graceful as she slowly bows out for the night.

She stood faithfully over us humans all day,
without demanding anything in return.

Every single morning at dawn,
she stands up and takes her position,
covering us with light, warmth and nutrients.
I always admired her,
especially her silent strength.

Sunset is especially beautiful
because she has such a delicate way
of saying goodbye for now.

Never has she scolded me
for not acknowledging her
or loving her in return.

I turned to you sitting beside me,
and you were lost in thought.
We agreed to meet here,
for we knew our time together had come to an end.

I thought back to how you fanned the flames
that have been smoldering in my belly
for hundreds of years,
and in this lifetime

you struck a chord, deep inside my soul.

Saying goodbye to you
feels like I am entering an asylum
for another hundreds of years
and my pain sends electric currents
throughout every corner of my consciousness.

Have I tricked myself
into believing you loved me at all,
since the mind is a very powerful instrument
in creating illusions?

You sat there silently,
tears slowly making their way down your face.

I dismissed every idea
that blazed through my mind:
that you loved me,
that you did not,
that you were confused...

I fought back my tears
like the fierce battlefield soldier that I am,
conditioned to tell no one
of the buckets of uncried tears
that are too scared to crawl out of my eyes
and tell you their names.

You never promised to love me,
and yet I still do not know
who is healing whom.

I will never be the same,
because for the first time in my life,
someone insisted that I be known.

Our relationship caused reorganization
deep in my psyche,
a healing borne
through my speechless pain.

You made me susceptible to being vulnerable,
somehow escaping detection
by the most faithful guards
in my zealous psyche.

The sun has now gone down completely,
and it is just you and I.

I summon up the courage to tell you
of my unspeakable pain at this separation,
but I am too weak.

Your presence has interrogated
my known limits of love for another human being,
and I am unable to extend the reach
of my personal frontiers for acceptance.

A turbulent and serene acceptance
that you are my exotic wound magnet,
the symbol that joins us in the wilderness
of our unconsciousness.

You knew I was abandoned and the orphaned,
and you returned the part that I needed the most:

the Passport of my Soul.

Glorious darkness, heightened creativity,
dances between my psyche and the ocean,
and no promises that I belong to you.

I open my eyes and you are gone.
In your place, you left me
the altarpiece I was desperately seeking,
and a key to open the aesthetic chamber
hidden far away
in my unknown wilderness.

I love you
for another hundred lifetimes,
and for today,
I know you will too.

It is because of the way you looked at me,
and all at once I knew
why you could not promise
to love me back.

You too, did not know
if you tricked yourself into believing
that I loved you truly.

For the mind
is a very powerful instrument
in creating illusions.

YOU ARE MY BEAUTIFUL UNIVERSE

This is you in my universe,
encasing me with your warmth,
your wisdom,
and your gentle compromise.

I know you are sleeping now
and a slight sadness has overcome me.

I always miss you when you sleep,
although I know
that you will cover me
with your kisses
at sunrise.

I gaze at your beautiful face
and breathe in rhythm with your breathing.
All my life I had dreamt of you,
and now it is just you and I
alone in our universe.

Promise me that when you awake,
you will take the pink rose I left you,
and you will caress it
against your soft and beautiful face.

Will you do so my beloved?

<u>*YOUR PROMISE TO ME*</u>

*This is where I wrote you my last letter,
asking you to remove the veil
covering my heart.*

*I whispered the words to you as I wrote them,
breathing them out through the window.*

*I cannot tell if you heard me,
because I am weary from a lifetime
of running and hiding
my sensitive and wise heart.*

*I do not know if you can understand
what it is like to be on the run for decades,
a terrified orphan alone in the wilderness.
But something happened to me
the day you called me your own.*

*I discovered a little house inside of me
and I made it
my Ark of Love,
calling it by your first name.*

*Your name always promises
to quiet my frightened heart,
and blows a spirit of Divine power
into my tender, sensitive self.*

*Now that I looked into
your beautiful, mystical eyes,
now that you have heard my cries,*

my words, my joyful song and dance,
can you swear
to feel my words from this little home?

Let them reach you,
and caress your beautiful face.

Will you pause
to whisper my name in the wind?
Promise me, my forever Love,
that I will never be lost to you.

Promise me this
or else a part of me will die,
and no one else can awaken her.

Will you, my beloved?

OUR MIDNIGHT PROMISE

The clock has struck midnight,
and I have arrived here,
our secret meeting place.
It is just you and I
as we had promised each other.

My love for you keeps me up at night.
I feel as awake by midnight
as I have in the early sunrise.

Thoughts of you and the mystical corners
inside your mind reel me in,
and I must obey my curiosity.

Standing here with you,
my beloved,
I have little to say,
because in your quiet and regal presence
you have already kept your word.

Ancient promises of keeping close to my heart,
and I trust in your quiet strength.

Speak no words to me,
for your gaze is all-powerful.

If we can be in-love throughout Eternity,
can you promise to warm me by your Flame?

It is you and only you
that can pierce past lifetimes of battle gear,

and leave footprints of gentle song
along my path.

Will you sing for me sweetheart?
as I sleep tonight?

I WAS BORN IN YOUR TEARDROP

I sing your praises every day
because you gave me life.

I saw in you the depths of life
encompassing the infinite sea of rage
that you so gallantly tried to hide from me.

Riding such deep red waves,
I struggled along to keep up with your distance.
I could not find you or catch my breath,
so I sat by the river
panting and gasping for a straw of life.

You troubled me,
because your song was so elusive,
so promising yet so chaotic.

I walked a very lonely
and frightened path around you,
forever terrified of your distance.
I danced around your angry hues,
and raised my head awaiting
the great ram's horn to tell me
he was now waiting for me.

Can't you understand my red fire
burning in your direction?

Why oh why can you not respond to my call?
You leave me here alone in my bundle of sufferings
all intertwined with your name.

You do not care for my calling –
just that I shall be your servant
for needs that are needless and endless.
You call my name,
and then dry my tears as if you truly saw them.

I cannot continue this running,
and I cannot sustain my breath,
for you have stolen the last bit of gold in my mind.
I stole it for you; I ran for you,
I ducked the hailstorm just to be with you.
And you so callously rigged my footsteps
to always come running back to you.
How could you be so mindless,
with a heart that screams my song,
but is empty and desolate after all.

Heed my cry, Beautiful and Troubled Soul:
I can run no more,
and I can hide no more
my depth of having been buried
by your empty deceit.
I longed and sought for you,
but I was just a birth
in your teardrop.

You cannot see me from afar
and you cannot embrace me from up close,
and so I will run far away,
back to the lonely desert from which I hail.

After all, I was born in your teardrop
and that is all that mattered.

You love me not,
and I can no longer embrace your face.

Be peaceful, be gone,
and be done with my memories.

Lonely hearts you will forever break,
and I was nothing
but a single drop in your rain.

SAY SOMETHING FROM ACROSS THE OCEAN

Sitting here alone at my desk,
ink, parchment and feathers waiting to be used
in service of my aching heart.

I tried to write in our unfinished diary,
but you said it is okay to say goodbye,
and I'm not crying.

But something inside of me is crying,
and I do not know her name.

I rise from this old wooden desk,
heavy and soaked with the tears of poets long gone.
In everything I never told you,
this is my most guarded pain:
I stopped myself from hoping
that I belonged with you.

I silently beg you to say something
from across the ocean.
A flock of birds flew past my window,
and I blew my hope to fly with them.

I live alone in a small room
at the top of an ancient and lonely castle.
The psyche and the Ocean are my closest friends,
for both have taught me their secrets.

I walked out of the orphanage I was left in
many moons ago,
the orphanage where I met you,

and at long last
fell so deeply in love with you.

Do you remember our first conversation,
where we found the symbol
that joins us in the wilderness?

You said you found a lonely poet in me,
and I could not understand you.

You said that you saw a beautiful dance
in the dark desert night with me,
and our secret knowledge
would carry us across the ocean,
and nothing
would remove this bond between us.

You were the passport of my Soul,
the death of an old friend,
my loneliness, and my reflection
of the glorious darkness:
our creativity, rage, intensity,
and love of the magical fire.

Do you remember all those nights
we sat by the bonfire, and reflected
on the mystery, paradox
and horizon of the cosmic soul?

You were my deepest celebration,
and I have created for you
an Altar Piece inside my heart.

After we parted from each other
I continued to seek for all that is beautiful,
and I still continue to find you in many lifetimes.

Never will I let you go,
and I still find myself calling out to you
to say something to me
from across the ocean...

BURIED ALIVE

Buried alive I struggled to peek
through this buried bonfire.

Alone and lost
through the underground of your heart,
I seek to find an escape.

Why can I not forge
a secret escape to the wild open,
away from your desperately reaching arms?

I thought I had run from you,
almost alone and free,
but I helplessly continue
to seek you all around me.

Every time I find myself
in your buried underground,
I am warmed by an untold bonfire,
not of human nature,
and untouched by humanity.

It was only I that touched it,
and from such a touch
this book of love poems has been born.

I can no longer ask you if you remember me,
if you seek me, if you take flight into
the unknown wild territory,
searching for me.

I did all that in the wild, hungry days of my youth,
and I still found you.
I cannot stop my roaring deafness,
for it permeates my whole entity.

For you have stolen my soul,
and have left me with only pieces of a memory.

You have crumbled my shame,
depleted my lies,
and ran with my tale.

Where are you now?
I humbly assert the demons inside me,
but they only answer me
with gremlins of dead poets,
forsaken lovers,
and lost memories.

I cannot get you out of my mind
because I have become your mind.

I cannot leave your heart,
because I have become your heart.

BEAUTIFUL, WOUNDED SOLDIER

Where are you now,
my beautiful, wounded Soldier?
I am you and I am still holding on to your name.

It lies on the bottom of my ocean,
collecting stories, raging fires,
and dying embers.

You ran from me once.
I ran from you.
And in our darkness
we are left with the desire for none at all,
and everything in middle.

Can you tell my story when I am gone?
When the winds blow the stories of my pages,
the leaves rustle like a hundred stomping soldiers,
and the battle cry is dying down.

Come whisper my name,
and sit beside me.

Do you remember this wounded soldier,
and can you hear my rush of tears
that turned into a timeless roaring river?

When you first met me,
you knew that this river was powerful enough
to propel us down to the very edges
of a never-ending love story.

This is a love story that sings
of how we together pulled eternity to us,
binding us forever with black and red hearts
of the wounded and beautiful brave.

You are my sadness, my grief,
my solitude, my unspeakable loneliness,
the depth of my joy, and the height of my hope.

I have loved you once before,
and you know I will return,
in every incarnation,
to deliver my books of love poems written
to carry us back into that spiritual fire.

Do you remember this fire,
where in the pit only Sadness and Love
can finally speak of their woes?
Where we gave rise to the birth of our emotions,
their lives, and the pain
that we birthed alone?

Fly alongside me,
my beautiful winged soul mate,
but do not look down
for fear that once again
you will be robbed by my heart.

I will swoon in
and capture you with my gaze,
and all stories from poets' past
will run and cry our names.

They will exclaim to the villagers
that our love has never been enough,
and can never have a name.

For you and I are alone in this capture,
both forever the captor and the captive,
forever seeking Higher.

I did love you once,
but now I am old and tired,
and I fear you may have long forgotten my name.
I have not yours.

I still dance and play inside your chest,
warming my tired, weary soul
against the heat of your magnificent bonfire.
See why now you cannot grab hold
of words and reason,
and you cannot stop singing my name.

You keep returning to the battlefield,
and lay flowers
for your beautiful, wounded Soldier.
I hear you cry, laugh and sing every time.

You have not forgotten me.

REMEMBER ME

Small in height, without a voice,
an unknown and silent face;
I turned to you for your memory of me.
You said you had none,
that I was unknown by you.

You screamed your darkness at me
and said that before me
I must always carry your burden.

Mute and broken,
I carried on with your baggage
blinded by my unknown pain.

I strengthened myself by our separation,
for many untold miles were ahead of me.
I trudged this desert alone,
calling your name
with an ache that screamed for endless miles.

I dared not speak to anyone
of this dark circle
you have burned in my middle,
for fear they would tie me
to your mad darkness
and call me your own.

Often, when the peace and white snow fell upon us,
I sailed down the mountain
and gazed into the dark blue night sky.

She was my true Mother,
and covered me in her blanket of love.

The blanket that you had forgotten
by that tall, forbidding doorway.
That was our last moment
as I became too small for your rage.

Through that doorway,
your forbidden rage
blew evil, dark winds at me.

Then I turned and walked away from it all,
into my own cave
of red, black and dark blue sadness.

You knew what you had done:
drove me to this brink of desolate nothingness,
with no more roses of life
to stand beside me.

Then came the most beautiful colorful River,
and she called me by name,
and embraced me with joy!

She lifted me up, twirled me around
and said she was invisible until I could see.

Many moons and beautiful angels
have twirled before me,
blanketed me
and shone their light ahead of me.

I saw you, but briefly.
I came back here today to tell you
that I still stand by your doorway,
as you try to scream your madness towards me.

But I have been sought by River's Light,
and she has never stopped calling my name.

I have become the Light,
not because I could see –
but because she refused to allow me
to sink into your despair.

I have come today, to return your baggage;
so heavy and false
that you have claimed as mine.

For no more shall I cry for you,
or roll your endless stones
in front of me.

A river of light comes
and claims me
as her true Daughter.

It is with Light
that I am now living an everlasting relationship.

Your seeking of Darkness
has lost its meaning.
I am Her Son,
Her Daughter,
and her True Child.

Your greatest lie hid my ultimate liberation,
and forever will I become
Her one and only.

I have become part of the Light.

Whenever I cry for you
by the tall, dark doorway
I do not cry because of how you broke me;
I cry because you lied to me, saying
if I left you to seek Her,
She would never love me back.

THE LIGHT IN MY DOORWAY

Soft rivers
happily, dance their way through
the endless earth,
following its paths and seeking life.

This is where
my footsteps have covered
the scattering of seeds you have left
for me to follow.

I sang songs for you,
hoping you would catch the notes
I left for you.

Long days have passed,
yet I cannot stop yearning for you.

Our love creates
such a mystery between us,
knowing neither words, nor God,
not any knowledge
of what supports our bond.

I still pray for you,
and when I dip my feather
in the intense black ink,
I know you are watching behind me.

The rushing roar of a nearby waterfalls
colors my broken arrow
with hopes of your gentle voice.

The water gently proceeds down the mountain,
taking her time.

She knows she is regal and beautiful,
and will hurry for no one.

She will flow when she is ready,
as the rocky path
feels right against her body.

I need to visit her
because she teaches me the grace
of moving through the roughness,
the lost madness I once had,
and the vast unknown.

I will slowly tell you of my first love,
and the madness I once endured.

I will run and forget you,
yet never will I stop writing
how you screamed to me of your darkness,
and how the Light
adopted and crowned me
as Her own.

How could you split me
between the Darkness and the Light,
forgetting how such despairing aloneness
has captured all other Vultures like you?

I have sought to know how I was shaped,

and who is my true being.

You kept trying to cover me
with your blanket of darkness.

I have not fallen prey to this tragedy,
and I kept the violet, singing her songs
throughout my dark sojourn
away from your disruptive lies.

Because of you,
I have disastrously misunderstood people
and the kind world at large.

Your tales were unsatisfactory for me,
and I had to pursue my distance
until the Light restored me from her opposite.

On my run I desperately grasped for solutions:
How can I encounter Love
and yet still remain at a safe distance?

Dissatisfied with the cactus-filled desert,
shedding your deceptions,
I sought an answer from your opposite.

Standing at the doorway;
at long last,
I have forgotten your language.

My thoughts of the Light
have become my language,
and no longer can I conceal Her.

THE FORGOTTEN FIREFIGHTER

I was born
in your chaotic, loud, disruptive mess,
lost in the sea of your preoccupied
and forever lost mind.

My self, yearned for differentiation,
but you provided me with no heritage,
only rigidity and chaos.

I became your Firefighter:
a tall, brave, and powerful rescuer.

I had to flee
from your screaming darkness,
escape from where there was no escape.

So I carried my extinguisher wherever I went,
and instinctively eradicated
the constant firing patterns
that came from you.

Without a face or my own name,
I sought to escape from you,
and I have,
only to discover
that decades ago
you trapped me without ropes.

Do you remember that day?
That day when I lost my name to you?

I have forever remained in a state
of seeking to love those
who hate and punish like you.

In seeking love from the unloving
I have both lost and found myself.

When I encountered
"the she" that I am mentioning,
her fire set all things ablaze.

So many paths and roads I have crossed,
eager to annihilate with my hose
the fire that could blind me.

Why do you always find me?
Or am I always searching for you?
Perhaps now my sadness will dissolve
this pitied alliance
and your enduring betrayals
will no longer separate me from
Her real love.

Yes, I know it was you who has encoded in me
your tragic warfare,
and I have believed it
to be my own rescue operation.

But you were no soldier –
only a deserter,
a wanderer in a state of madness.

I have claimed you, because I had no choice,

but to rescue you from perpetual drowning.

I kept forcing myself to be as the light,
hoping you would look at me and say:
"My true battle has been won!"

But you just remained
forever seeking in your endless loss.

May these ghosts finally rest in the light.

My memories of you
and the Forgotten Firefighter
need you no longer.

Love has coached me through her beautiful gates,
and I will forever be in her sanctuary.

Your jealous rage
will not deter me
from my new mission:
to seek my lost eyes and see forever more.

THE CHILD
THAT IS THE MOTHER OF THE WOMAN

I climbed the stairs in our old town house,
looking for your trail.

Loose papers flew towards me,
danced in front of me, urging me
to continue climbing.

Ancient candles blew, whispering your secrets,
forbidding me to continue my ascent.

Echoes of your beautiful singing
bounced on the walls
asking what was stopping me.

I heard his silence,
and my fear trapped me once again.

You both screamed your nothingness at me,
and wanted all I had.

To comfort my weary heart,
I allowed
the strings of light and harmonious music
grow deep down into my abyss,
and comfort she that was inconsolable.

I could not speak with you –
I could only feel your claws dripping with blood,
constantly seeking for revenge.

Your madness has been incomprehensible,
and you have thrown dirt
on the graveyard
of the pieces of my mind.

I climb these stairs
to come back and seek for you,
so I can drag the isolated and neglected child
out of her piece
of your graveyard.

I must show her, this child
who is the mother of the woman,
that a light exists past the hallway,
and together
we shall make the ascension.

No longer will your crazed madness
alienate myself from this child,
and no longer will Love be unreal.

For you, I had to invent another self,
this Mother-Child,
so we can both survive your cruel tyranny
of closeted darkness.

My despair has dragged me out
into a world of freedom and courage,
and as I march uniquely forward,
I leave both yours and his screams behind me.

This mask of mine
continues to disintegrate

the further I climb these stairs,
until I can feel the Divine touch.

Bright light rushes towards me,
as I have reached the top of the stairwell.

I no longer hear you,
but I have acknowledged all of this and that,
both my own darkness of rage,
and your own.

I stop here,
because I know that this Light
has endured with me,
and has kept Her promise to take me,
save me, redeem and
bring me out of your gates
of screaming hell.

"What is your name?!", a voice called out of me.

And I replied:
I am the child that once was
the mother of the woman,
who owes everything
to the Light.

THE FIRST TIME I STOOD BEHIND YOU

I decided today,
in the circle of my fear,
to get behind You.

You have forever been my true love,
my rock
and
fierce protector.

I have spent so much time and soul
fearing your abandonment of me.

Today I stood behind You,
and my life-long fear
lost its way.

OUR LOVE CAN NEVER END:
SECRET MADNESS FROM A COLORFUL FIRE

Twelve long years have gone by,
and I find myself
alone in the deep woods
of my mind.

I have told her repeatedly
how fearful I am
that the one I yearn for
may not exist.

Women dance and laugh
around the bonfire,
singing tales
of my fears gone by.

In the churning,
brilliant embers
of my unconscious,
I face the Shaman's messenger alone.

She repeats to me in secret whispers:
to touch, hold and allow my deepest
most intense turmoil
to flow through my fingers.

The one I am yearning for
will walk behind me,
and touch my back
in a gesture of life and love.

I will be grounded
in all that is wild, free and true.

I am on this walk
fearful and fearless:
terrified of her reign of non-existence –
yet living in wild freedom
that no one or everyone
might steal from me.

"Continue to walk along
the pinecone path I have left for you",
she whispers.

"For your seeking lends great hope
to the lost, neglected and isolated.
You must confront the whirlwind you fear, loathe,
and cherish all at once.
The beloved that you fear and seek,
is both you and they.
And they can speak to you and through you.
Jump, laugh, and cry her name.
She knows her own name,
and it is through yours
that she hopes to be seen."

I walk on through
the deep and mysterious woodlands
of my unconscious.
My own madness, success and failure
have their own names, faces, and life.

No more are these strange parts of our darkness,

but familiar secrets
none wish to endeavor to see.

I am not unique in myself
only a nameless, colorful,
searing fire
illuminating what no one wishes to see
through their own eyes.

I am still seeking the beloved I fear does not exist,
and all roads lead me back to her,
seen through my very own.

I KEEP FORGETTING
AND REMEMBERING YOU

I left this morning on my boat,
and let it drift
to the middle of a beautiful ocean.

This is the place where I return,
because she holds my secrets, tears,
and colorful promises.

Many moons have set over this spot,
and I still cry
remembering and forgetting you.

I have encountered and trusted so many,
but of all, you have taught me
about a love so unearthly,
that I must tell you what happens
when I think of you.

I remember the day I tried to find you,
but you were already gone.

I am not a chaser when it comes to love,
because a long time ago
love was my god
and ripped too many
bleeding tears from my heart.

She left in her wake a hole
that only God can fill.

*I have long abandoned my needs
and quest for love –
my mind does its job of protecting me
from such a pitiful downfall.*

*When I would think of love,
the broom in my head immediately
swept it all away,
and I tightened my armor.*

*Then you came along
from out of the cosmos.*

*The stars decided
when it was time for us to meet,
and since then you have flamed a candle
deep inside my silence.*

*You never told me where you went to,
and I still cry over your name.*

*You often send me messages,
and when I read them,
I cannot help, or explain the tears
that gently fall down my face.*

*I entered the spiritual world
for answers and stories about how we got here,
and how we will be drawn to each other
again and again.*

*When you first left,
I did not understand*

your language or your message.

I knew you were speaking to me,
because I was haunted
by your still, small voice.

You have taught me
how to listen and connect,
and I lost my loneliness.

My passions have instructed me
to keep remembering you,
even though human weakness
keeps me so very young and immature.

I keep forgetting and remembering you,
because you were over my head.

You removed my veils
revealing how little
I actually know about love.

In doing so, my pain revealed
a poet's cove of treasures
made up of prolific words, tears,
scarred ink and parchment.

What I fear the most
is that you will wake me up, and say
this was all my dream:
that you have long said good bye,
that the messages were all my own.

But my Divine source has been telling me
that my essence is of the Poet and Lover.

Every now and again I feel your embrace,
pointing me to the exact spot
where God has put me to stand.

Thank you my true Spiritual Master.

You speak so deeply into me,
and all I can do is sit here
in the center of the ocean
and watch the beautiful sunset.

It is time to say good-bye and turn around.

I hope that you read this letter,
and know that I am incapable
of giving up on you.

Perhaps one day
you will be joining me here on this boat,
and you will say that indeed this love
has been from God.

I have no other way to explain
this unending river of beautiful colors
that sings her way
from my heart to yours.

WHY I WRITE

Music is what feelings sound like,
and when I write creatively,
I am guided by this music.

That is what I hear
and the words
just run off my fingers,
eager to settle in the pages
and make themselves at home.

INSANITY

I had two experiences with such insanity.

*The first experience
broke my heart,*

*and the second one
awakened it.*

I STAND WHERE GOD PUTS ME

*The hole in my heart
has gotten smaller;
this happens every time
I think of you.*

*I found out tonight
that you have been
God's gift to me all along.*

*You have led me
not to an endless drowning sunset
for lovers
who cannot separate,
but you have led me
to the trenches
of my own unconscious.*

*It was deep in these trenches
that I faced my deepest fear:*

*that the beloved I am longing for
will leave me,
or does not exist.*

*I cried, fought and pulled away,
but you kept reminding me
that all that will be after this process
is Love, only Love.*

*I have tried so long,
on my own,*

to reach inside my own silence,
and all I could find
was my torn-to-pieces hood.

My passions have instructed me to tell you,
in all my vulnerability,
what I fear the most.

I thought you were God Herself
because my mind was just doing her job;

now I must step back and accept
that you are my beautiful Guidepost.

I am helpless in the face of
the plays that take place dramatically
in my unconscious.

You repeatedly show up
in every place I hide,
in my nighttime dreams,
daydreams and in every corner
where I run and seek
my own special symbols.

Why are you always there,
telling me that you never left?

You are my portion of Love,
my special symbol of our calling
here on Mother Earth.

I fight to accept

the rawness of my sensitivities,
and I stand where God puts me.

Has God
placed you
in the same standing place,
next to me?

INFINITE MADNESS OVER YOU

You called on me
just as I was switching my hiding place,

and without knowing you,
without the stories my mind tells me,
without the touch of your gentleness,
I followed you.

When you left
I continued to wander
throughout the wild, generous forest
calling out to you.

I could not hear back from you,
because the fierce ocean swallowed you up.

I saw you lost at sea,
alone in your small and lonely boat,
still and crying in middle of the dark night.

You put up your barriers so I could not see you,
and you could not see my pain
at knowing how lost and terrified you are.

I wrote you a letter,
rolled it up in a scroll
and let it drift out to sea.

I asked everyone
who encountered your stormy seas
if they saw my letter delivered to you.

One kind man took pity on us,
and said he would ensure
that you received it.

I smiled and thanked him
for helping me stop
this infinite madness over you.

I shall know you once again,
tonight at midnight,
when the moon shines through my bedroom window
spelling out the message that you had left me.

With the Great Sun's permission,
tomorrow morning,
I shall write you again.

Until then,
do not let the rocking boat,
stormy dark seas,
and lonely isolation
fool you into deceit that you are
unloved and abandoned.

Where you live today is only the story
you keep telling yourself tomorrow.

THE ROSE GARDEN AS OUR WITNESS

I went for a walk this evening
in a beautiful rose garden,
gently touching the roses as I walked by.

Along my path,
I saw The Wanderer approach me,
with a special glow around him,
and a weariness that told of his days ending.

We sat down together on the bench,
and he asked me what was bothering me.

I said that I never completely got over you,
and that I had left a part of my soul with you.

A tear rolled down his cheek,
as The Wanderer has always been by my side,
through lonely desert travels,
and magical trips around the world.

Faithful and gentle he always was,
and now it is his calling
to return to the Infinite Light.

It is time for us to say good-bye, and yet,
neither of us
can bear such a separation.

He asked me what bothered me most
about having lost you,
and I said that you instructed me

to first share my soul
in order to touch the world
with my words.

Once I find out who answers,
I will wait for them by the old fig tree,
and they will hand me a secret letter.

"Why does this frighten you", he gently asked me.
I replied, holding back my river of frozen tears:

"This requires me to go
to where I have rarely even gone myself.
No one but you has ever suggested that,
and if they did, I was not listening."

"Go deeper and find out
what lays beneath this fear"
he gently tugged at me.
I am morbidly terrified
of what I will find
when I go there!

Would I bump into
my ancient nursery-room ghosts
roaming free?

Would they be hungry or thirsty?
Would they recognize me?
What would they shout out to me?

What if my ghosts are
walking around blind

169

and bumping into all my wounds?
Would I expect this person to find and fix them?
And if I am not loved back,
can I survive the lonely psychic pain
I am sure to endure?

These haunting questions came out
and I held back nothing.

It is time now to let these deep insecurities
breathe the Light of God
and receive Her Infinite Unending Love.

I am ready now.

I felt the roses blow kisses at me,
filling our garden with a soft gentle light.

I could see The Wanderer depart from this world,
and I cried and clung on to him,
in terror of our separation.

These were his final words as he was departing,
and I share them now with you.
But promise me
that you too will hold these words sacred,
and when you say them to yourself,
come sit beside us in the rose garden.

Here many sacred conversations
have taken place,
and many fears
were washed away

by The Wanderer's
love and wisdom.

"You were once part of the Great God,
all of us were One Soul.

We were separated and divided
and took the form of Human Beings,
flesh and blood.

You still carry a part of this Great Soul,
your forever mirror and original soul mate.

Seek from her wisdom, and remember
that genuine Love
is everlasting and eternal.

Seek to share what comes from here
and you will know the rest".

How do I know this to be true?

From my years during exile
when I fiercely guarded my nursery,
I discovered I was
a part of something
ancient and magical.

The Wanderer took his last breath,
and I covered his beautiful, gentle
and wise eyes.

I covered his entire body in roses,

and left him to the love and care
of the rose garden.

As I walked away,
I whispered my promise to him.

This letter is a fulfillment of that promise.

You will know it
if you take time
to sit with me on the bench,
amongst the most beautiful of roses.

Will you sit beside me?

MUST I REMAIN CONSCIOUS?

I remember you,
but I do not remember you,
until you came to me in my dream last night.

I walked along the dirt road,
looking for the house
where you said you would meet me.

You did not show up;
in your place was my old school friend.

She said you spoke to her about me,
and told her
how your love for me was complete.

My heart felt that she was speaking the truth;
and I know you now,
as I have not known you before.

You left me in my place,
alone and in the dark.

I thought that only I loved you,
but indeed
you were doing the same for me.

I thought I was the expert,
and you were my subject.
But in fact, you were doing for me
what no one has done before.

As I was pondering all this,
you appeared before me with a beautiful smile,
a light that came from an ancient candle.

I sat there and felt the greatest pleasure,
a nirvana of emotions
that only the lonely poets speak about.

And at once,
all of my panic, psychic pain,
love and attachment to you
made complete sense.

I adored your beautiful smile,
and in a flash,
you were gone.

No apologies for leaving me,
no consideration of untold spoken words,
and your unbearable, unbreakable silence.

It suddenly got cold and dark all around me.
Mysteriously, I still cannot explain
what happened to me with you.

But it's power comforted me
as I watched in anguish
as you turned and walked away:

My severed ties to my creativity,
to an ongoing Spiritual Presence,
my fear that enslaved me
then released me,

and our primal bond;
all bore me fruit.

Your beautiful love and smile
turned my heart away from my fear,
to the ability to discover
what are only half-truths and hate
from counterfeit idols of love.

You inspired me
to release my delusions,
and you are the one person
who gave me an idea
that changed my entire life.

What remains behind my mask
is now being seen by the world.
Do you know the essence of who I am?

You asked me to share this
and my true yes to you
changed my life.

I held on to your scarf that you left behind,
and let my tears run rivers through it,
because that too
is my message back to you.

You said no
so I could say yes.

I FOUND YOUR SECRET ON 12-6-15

I laid my head down to sleep,
swept away from conversations
between Angels and their friends.

Outside my window
beautiful blue birds softly sang me bedtime songs,
and my breathing got heavier and heavier.

The owls stood watch
protecting me
from dangers of the night.

The wind blew,
swirling all around my home,
sending the message
that she is my fierce protector.

My mind was filled with you,
how complex we both are.

I pondered how I re-arranged
my entire emotional existence
having found then lost you.

My whole mind and spirit
was filled with the resolution
of you coming back
in a way that I can see, hear and understand.

I far from comprehend
these torments and ramblings of my heart,

yet you keep coming back to me.

I felt you at 3:00am,
as you sent me smoke signals from your heart,
and all at once
I found your secret.

You too cannot disobey the forces of love,
although we have both tried:
fierce, stubborn and passionate as we are.

At this moment,
I knew that my transformation
is a death of mind-confusing messages
that your love is not possible
or does not exist for me.

So I put on a colored coat
painted by your words,
so I can forever see your beautiful face
along the mirrors of my body.

I found your secret,
for it is my secret too:

the energy of true love
cannot be created or destroyed.

We are the ships, the ocean, and the sails
for each other's vessel.
Everything has now been settled,
and I am no longer estranged
from my sanity and insanity.

You are both for me,
and I still cannot rebel
against the forces of love.

We have both taught each other
that love is never a one-way mirror.

Can I take you away
from someone else
you were meant to love?

I gazed on the image of your face
and traced my name all over it.

So now you have my secret too.

DEEP BREATH OF MY SOUL
SHATTERED FALSE IDOLS ATTACHED TO ME

I took a walk
to the back wards of my mind,
where remnants
of my once-suffering self
used to live.

The dreary walls,
grey skies and dark shades
all reminded me
of what once was an existence
full of judgment.

Life with love and light
was incomprehensible to me,
and a feeling of normalcy
was out of my reach.

I did not want anyone's pity:
I wanted to be recognized
in my distinctiveness and differentness.

I wanted you
to teach me of my separateness
and not be threatened by my despair
and seemingly
endless loneliness.

I tried to speak,
but words eluded me.

I tried to cry
but the frozen entry way
refused to allow me access.

You cannot understand me
without understanding
the once-infinite despair
I experienced.

I needed to live here,
in the back wards of my mind,
because it was the only safe place I knew.
In retreat.

All of my self was looking
into a one-way mirror,
and I saw no darkness in myself.

I saw the reflection
of the darkness of others,
and this brought me
to a unified search for you.

All parts of me,
my own light and my own darkness,
crowded together, huddled in hope
and a sense of camaraderie.

They knew of a source of light,
but left me out of their discussions.

I pondered what their joy was all about,
but thought I had no ability to connect

to whatever they were hurriedly speaking of.

I looked out of my bleak window,
and was suddenly gripped with an ache
so I mustered the courage to ask you:

"Why do you want me to search for you?
I cannot forgive how hidden you are,
I cannot answer if you are alone or not,
and why when I ponder
how you can hide your love from me,
do I suddenly find myself
standing amidst the holy circle?"

I pondered this for a while,
and saw through the mirrors surrounding me,
that I always seek for you in places
you promised that you would not be.

In my youth, I was hidden,
overwhelmed by fear and sorrow.
You never intended to open the door to this room.
But that is how we found each other.

We took turns teaching each other
the futility of our broken teachings.

You saved me from secrets
that were keeping Shame
an unkind ruler over me.

You said that I did not have to spend my life
living in a secret fortress,

181

*and that we would take it down
brick by brick.*

*No longer a powerless slave,
I would let go of my own power
and exchange it
for the light and love of Hers.*

*I heal and heal more,
and continue to walk over the bridge,
freed from prison-walls.*

*Often I return to this room,
so I can pour my love
directly onto the bricks and spot
where I once lived.*

*She can let out that light
from her bleak bedroom window,
and call out no more false promises
to the gods and idols
that continually offer empty hopes
for counterfeit love.*

THE SACRED STORY OF NUMBER 11

I am a Storyteller who lives everywhere
and all over the ancient lands
of every soul with a voice.

I came here today because
The She whom I fear does not exist,
speaks to me using
exquisitely perfect writing tools,
sending me on all kinds of journeys,
with the promise to write it back home.

So here is my story when I encountered
the sacred Number 11.

I first met him when I rose to the next level,
seeking for the She that I fear does not know me.

It was one of my many encounters
with wrestling with the fusion that I discovered,
as I combated my humanity
and my earnest escape
through the circles of divine light.

He, this magical number 11,
invited me to his magnificent tent
made of blue diamonds.

Inside his tent,
there were 11 different
stunning and distinct incenses
in the shape of a crown.

I asked Number 11 why he brought me here,
why his number,
and why now.

He told me that it is because
I did not know where I came from,
and that for me to seek my Twin Flame,
I must stop worshipping
false images of love.

At first, I did not understand his comments to me;
after all, I was so protected
from such frightening ideas
of "love" and "intimacy",
I could not connect myself
to worshipping its' counterfeit.

He saw my hesitation and confusion,
and sat me down on one of the most beautiful
blue-diamond chairs.

"I am only a messenger for you,
and I have existed since
the dawn of human history.
I am a Hidden One,
and I am constantly seeking
those who seek for me.
They cannot hear, see or feel me,
and most refuse to believe anymore
in my righteous existence.
They have traded me for
their pain of holding back love,
and do not seek to be redeemed

from their suffering."

His words were settling inside me,
inside that pure tent of my light
that everyone knows we have.
It felt freeing to believe in him,
this odd but powerful creature.

As I sat in his stunning tent of light and color,
I felt lifted out of my insecurities,
doubts and beliefs that I am unlovable
and doomed to a life of isolation.

Sensing my freedom, he instructed me
to take my doubts, fears and insecurities
and place them
on one sparkling purple diamond.

He told me to take my hopes, dreams,
true beliefs and talents,
and place them on another orange diamond.

He showed me the magical red river of light
that connected them both,
and above the river
the following message appeared to me:
"Time and Oaths".

I stood up and thanked him,
this mighty Number 11,
and promised to keep returning
to our magical meeting place.

He whispered to me
that what I seek for
is hidden behind the number 11,
and that time will reveal to me
sacred oaths never sacrificed
nor forsaken over time.

I was comforted
as an infant gazing
into the soft smile of his beloved mother.

I knew that I must continue
to travel and tell of these stories,
for we human beings
are a band of lost and fragile sets of lovers.

Some speak of this Great Love,
some hide behind the stone
and hurl words of anger and fear,
and some are too scared to try.

I am all of them.

MY COVENANT WITH NUMBER 11

Today I took a swim
in the middle of the deep blue waters
that are near you.

I invited you to surface,
to pause for a deep breath,
but you pulled me back down.

You fiercely connected to me,
speaking of your aches,
pains and joys,
and showed me that you and I
are bound as one.

Repeatedly,
I tried to get us to surface,
as breath and sunlight were evading us.

You pulled me back down,
and said that you want us
to only remain here,
in the deep subconscious of our souls.

This is where I heard you say
that you made a covenant with Number 11
on behalf of both us.

These are experiences that you,
and only you,
have provided to me,
and I was speechless.

Is your love inauthentic
because you refuse to make it conscious,
impairing my ability to scream,
shout and dance to the world
of our love for each other?

Or are you pulling me down
so that I can fulfill
your primary hunger
for in-utero attachment
never fulfilled in your lifetime?

You said that you saw a fire in my eyes
that was terribly attractive to you;
both for its power
and its rule of potential destructiveness.

You tell me that you are too sensitive,
and long to be in a safe zone with me,
floating on a soft white cradle
without restraints,
distress, broken promises,
or vague expressions of love between us.

You called me your Heart's Magician –
do you remember that talk under the old fig tree?

You said that you recognize me
because you saw in me
your own identity.

You said that you were pretending
not to love me,

because we would otherwise
have to reveal ourselves to each other.

So you chose to flee from me
in the hopes that you would stop being so torn
by the fire you keep seeing in my eyes.

You said that we both have secrets and needs
that we urge to reveal to each other,
but you were trembling inside.

"Why are you trembling?" I asked you.

"Are you fearful of forsaking your secrets to me?
You fear that your truth is that
you hide behind your lie,
so you should not be irredeemably alone?"

So I share with you my favorite heartache:
I have already gone and claimed
your heart's most hidden inner territory,
and engraved my footsteps
in all of your hiding places.

I promised Number 11
that I would not let you lead me back
to where you splintered- to- bits
my secret hiding place.

My Beloved:
you are no longer pretending
to be what you are not,
and as you step out,

you have emerged
as a ghost of symbolic salvation.

What price must I pay
for admitting to you
that the only real death I have feared
is the revelation of my feelings
of love for you,
and the day you lost the crown
I placed on your head?

Everything else has already been settled.

Our love was already announced
before the King and Queen,
and our countrymen have graciously accepted
our covenant with the Number 11.

You made me aware
of the secretive power of Number 11,
but you have not yet given me permission
to weep over your cries
that only I can hear.

FORGIVENESS

But what exactly does *"forgive"* mean?

My favorite answer
is from a chief in Africa
when involved in making peace
between two war-torn tribes.
There was much violence and suffering
inflicted by one warring faction over the other.

*"Forgiveness
is the commitment not to take revenge."*

I extend his brilliant answer:
"not to take revenge
against anyone
INCLUDING myself."

There are many ways
in which we punish ourselves
for crimes we think we committed.

Indeed, some of us were convinced
we are guilty from inception
and seek to punish ourselves
through various means.

The most tragic self-revenge
is withholding love
for fear of being taunted.

Taunted by whom?

By the schoolyard bully
that romps around our mind
screaming
of our unworthiness and inferiority.

This resident of our mind
needs our forgiveness
more than all the outside demons of the world,
because his residence is the factory
of everything we see
played out on our life stage.

YOU HINTED WHAT I CONCEALED WITHOUT MY PERMISSION

I agreed to go down
to the basement of your mind
just the other day.

You lived in a house by the sea,
and as the sunset and waves roared their way
to night time,
you agreed to let me see
what you keep hidden.

None of your past lovers
were so persistent and determined
to understand your shell.

As I was descending the stairs,
I heard cries coming from the treasure chest.
It looked untouched
and permanently sealed.
I dared to approach
and gingerly opened it.

Suddenly and without warning,
papers began to fly out,
and a look of terror gave you away.
You have been keeping your secrets here
and in your conflict of inviting me,
I found your eleven hidden
silver keys of redemption.

For the decades of your living,

you kept what you found to be
undeliverable to humanity,
hidden here.

I had tried
so desperately
to love and own you,
misguided
by my own ignorance
of darkness and light.

I was preoccupied
with possessing the book, you gave me.
You concealed all this
by roaming freely;
devouring the pleasures
of the wild, open fields.

Your fear provoked
my unending curiosity and compassion.

You shook your head from side to side,
forbidding me
from going further,
but begging me to continue.

You have
numerous broken arrows
stuck within your chest,
and you gave me mine back.

When I touched your hand,
I saw a glimpse

of scattered flames all around us.

I suspect
that you are a fugitive on the run
from your own demons,
forever in exile,
roaming free to distance yourself
from blasts of wild, roaring oceans of love.

You are either a shepherd for the devil,
or a Queen of the Wild,
and you will have no one as your own.

When your beloved comes close,
you roar,
you melt into a weeping willow,
and you bite
with a furious taste for blood.

I feel my time has come to leave,
as I am terribly overwhelmed
and without answers.

I will light a fire
by the grave only you and I know of.
I laid my head against the gravestone,
now my pillar standing loyally in his place.
I fell asleep for a great many hours,
the most I ever had.

For I had forgiven you completely,
the moment I sat down on the box
you have been carrying

and pulled you against me
for an embrace.

That was my awakening
from the Great Northern Wind.
You have entered with me
to this great space of love and truth,
for I have found
what you have been trying to say
all along:
when you see my face,
you let your heart light up,
and know
that I am the carrier
of both the light and the dark.

Or perhaps to you
I am just another mirror
along the walk
of seeking the broken pieces
of your completeness.

Oh My Beloved,
You are my beautiful evening spirit,
and this site is now holy ground.

I called you to my existence,
and for now,
I must let you go.

You taught me what I needed to learn.
Yet, without my permission,
you found all that I had concealed.

I can only love you
until we are both resting in peace
along this mysterious graveyard.
And then I will reach for you
once again,
to begin this journey for all eternity.

Sleep well my beautiful evening Queen.

And yes,
I do keep your photograph
by my side.

I never forsake my promises.

SOULS ARE UNITED BY PAIN

Souls are united by pain.
This is why I think
I fell in love
with the most broken-hearted.

So I can face my own,
and collect the gold hidden
in the trenches of my own unconscious.

My lovers were all messengers,
but I tricked myself into believing
I was there to rescue them.

And I think they were compassionate enough
to allow me such trickery,
so that finally I can find some peace
within my own brokenness.

DENIAL: MY ONCE-SLAVE MASTER GONE WITH THE WAVES OF TRUTH.

I fought waves and waves of anxiety
to swim to the truth.
When I finally reached
the shores of my truth,
I saw my most intense fears
float past me.

And that is when I discovered
that denial is the father of anxiety.

Not as a character defect
of not trusting God
or any other moral failing.
Just that I owned up
to some pretty deep darkness
once-surrounding me.

I am free and live a life of truth,
and I will never again
be enslaved by denial.

GENUINE SELF

You may never be fully comfortable
living inside your skin,
until you are aware of your true self,
and your choices are based on
your honest discovery.

What is ailing you and in what area?
Do you live a meaningful life?
It has taken me
a full 40 years to reach this place
and then proceed to accept it.
This is the developmentally appropriate age
and people reach this place
unique to their personal path.

And of course,
to how awake they can be.

I can never
and will never
go back to being asleep.

My sleep was self-protective,
and since no longer necessary,
I am dedicated to remain awake.

200

LOVE

Love is so important to our existence.
We come from Love,
and we look for it
slipping and sliding,
like a child learning to ski for the first time.

Without the intention
to break anyone else,
we so often end up broken ourselves
in this process.

I, too, have been on both sides.
I have sought forgiveness,
and I have forgiven.
And for that I am at peace,
because I have truly understood
and accepted that I alone
am Love.
And for this present moment,
that is enough.

THICK STAGE CURTAINS

I fell in love with your soul,
and all the characters
you carefully placed on the stage.

Behind the thick stage curtains
you sat in silence,
too insecure to tell me
what you really need.

That you had no more energy left to cry,
and did not know
how to dance on stage
looking them in the eye.

That your heart was so drenched
with secrets and screams
that forced your tears underground,
where no one else dared to go.

You would seduce
anyone who tried to pull back the curtains,
and charm them far away
from the curtains entrance.

I sat in the audience
and watched you with a smile,
as tears ran down my face.

I saw it all,
and I loved all of you,
but you were too frightened

to look in my direction.

I'm still here, my love,
somewhere in the audience
where you cannot see me
from where you are.

And when you are ready
to put down your tired mask,
and open your stage curtains,
there you will find me too.

ILLUSIONS

It is easier to protect your illusions,
than face the pain
that forced you
to create these illusions
when you had nothing else.

IF YOU TURN AROUND, THIS ROSE
I WILL GIVE YOU

Dancing in my playground
twirling and breathing in the pine forest air,
I gaze far away into your memory.

This is my favorite playground,
where I console myself
by seeing you here with me.

A playground where our demons
play hide-and-go-seek with each other,
and you and I are free
to face each other once again.

You whisper in my ear:
"is this real, but can it last?"

I dance away from you,
leaving candied red rose petals
along the path.

You run and chase me,
but you run much faster than I am skipping.
I can never keep up with you,
and I whisper so loud
I awaken the sleeping forest.

I wish for you to slow down,
but you keep on running.
I carve my question on a regal pine tree
hoping you will find it:

"this love you say you seek in us:
is it love or is it barter?"

Both of our questions left unanswered
as we run in opposite directions.
How did it get this way?

We heard each other shout
that our hearts are bound in chains
from the moral narcissism
we learned in our father's house.

We do not chase love,
because we honor
our individual family legacy
of deceitful withdrawal,
without knowing
how ignorant and lonely
we are in this matter.

It is only here in our magical forest
that I feel free
to speak all this to you.

We both know that the gentle trees
protect our secrets fiercely.

I have tried to speak of these things to you,
but you wear a mask
and you smile
through your beautiful and sad eyes.

I see your mask as a trap,

and your eyes as a deep river
I keep plunging myself into.

I swim in your dark
and furious waters,
gasping for air,
until I find the latch of your trap door.

I must turn the handle
and risk what is inside,
perhaps a heart with no sun.
Or can I remain here
forever looking for your echo?

I chose, instead,
to go very deep inside myself
to hold back from either of them.

If you can reach me here,
you can see
this beautiful red rose I am holding.

If you turn around,
I will give it to you.

WHERE DO I END
AND YOU BEGIN?

Everything rests for a moment
as you pose for a photo.

You have deceptive eyes,
after years and years
of hiding your torment,
and ignoring the suffering
of those that adored you.

I stare at your now-still photo,
coaxing my demons to remain outside,
or they would not allow me
this silence.

You ripped up my last letter to you
in anger,
and you never noticed
my empty chair.

So every morning,
I follow my ritual of singing with the birds,
smelling the wild roses,
and deeply breathing in
the pure pine forest air.

The gifts of nature
are my meaningful rewards,
as I so often felt on the brink of death
by forces unseen,
wondering why

you were never home for me.

He, who was supposed to protect me,
was lost and operating
from behind
his noxious mask.

And somehow through all of this,
you and I were both
rescued by the Shadows.

This is how we had come to greet each other.
Perfect strangers all through the night,
and then you were gone,
and all I had was the fire
behind the black triangle.

I listened as your silent footsteps
made their way down the hall,
and all at once,
I was the orphan
with rich patterns of pain, creativity,
and depth of soul
I had not yet touched.

I cried for you,
but the fires of your selfishness
drowned out my calls
for your love.

I hoped you would decide
not to deceive and abandon me,
and that you would come back for me.

As I lay cold and shaking in the orphanage,
I never stopped looking for you.
Would you come searching for me,
child-by-child, bed-by-bed,
crying out my name?

No, that never happened,
and I am forever lost in the classroom
trying to find you.

My comforts are
the gentle, kind forests
and powerful rivers
running side by side,
wild children of the summer,
the magical classroom under the sea,
and the yellow bassinet I fiercely guard.

The crib and the cave,
this is where my ghost continues roaming,
hoping you will love me once more.

I never slept until I wept for you,
and only the pyramids that I climbed
gave me strength to move
beyond your memory.

I wished, oh so desperately,
that you would write me back,
perhaps just to soften my landing,
as I hold still,
staring into

your deep and troubled eyes.

Can you tell me please?
where do I end
and you begin?

I TRIED TO SAVE YOU

I met you long ago,
when we were carefree young fearless souls.

You told me of your secrets
and where to find the golden key,
and I told you mine.

We swore
never to reveal it to anyone
but each other,
time and time again,
and in every lifetime.

We kept appearing
in each other's dreams,
accidental encounters,
and echoes from across
universes and lifetimes.

But in this lifetime, things were different.

We were each stuck
on pieces of broken grief,
jagged, rough
and impossible to walk on.

We each laid out a road for each other,
but the bricks were too hot to touch,
and the Sun told us
it was not yet time.

In our encounter,
your cries snuck past
my secret, locked doors,
and you let yourself
in to my sacred darkness.

I toughened up,
put on my strongest armor,
withdrew my sword,
and was ready to battle you.

I tried to save you,
but really,
I was trying to save myself.

I allowed myself
to fall in love with you every time
I saw your face.

In your eyes, I saw a She
who is still ruled by her demons.

I tried to lift my sword,
but it melted in my arms.

I tried to tell you
how my grief for you
is never ending,
but instead,
I flew my ghosts in formation
pointing towards
the whispers of my soul.

Why must you have
such darkness in your eyes,
and why must I completely surrender
my love for you?

I was born in her darkness,
and thought I was born blind.

For so many years, I walked through life
squinting in the dark,
believing I was only
a Child of the Darkness.

I am still afraid of you,
because you hold on to your pain:
raw, cut and bleeding,
you are a stubborn mirror.

Your ongoing silence
has opened up many doors of light for me,
and because you refuse to join me
in the playground of the light,
I have been redeemed from
a desolate and agonizing exile.

When you are ready, my love,
you will know where to find me.

I am always waiting for you
to join me in the grassy fields,
where my open heart will rain
endless storms of light

upon both of us.

But for now,
you still remain afraid,
and I remain a freed prisoner
from death's most devious traps.

You were the hand that drew me out,
and I shall follow you around lifetimes,
trailing ribbons of light
we once vowed only for each other.

I MISTOOK YOUR LOVE FOR GOD, WORSHIPPING YOU INSTEAD

Deep in the black woods I go often
to cleanse my breath,
wondering how you came into my heart
with such finality.

After the eleven pyramids I climbed:
hot, sweaty and in dire need of nourishment.

The beautiful black triangle
kept calling me home,
but I rigged the climb
so I would come see you.

When I approached the top,
there was a circle of eleven triangles,
and each spoke a different message to me.

The first one instructed me
to seek inside myself
for the Good Mother, in all of us,
who was there waiting for me.

The last triangle spoke
of the Man inside all of us,
the hero on his horse and mighty sword,
that refuses to surrender at all.

And the other nine of them
coached me to sit outside the world,
and seek the Divinity in her eyes

that was everywhere.

I sat amongst them,
but all I could think was wondering
when you were coming home.

Why would these holy and perfect triangles
seek me?
I felt like an orphan in an empty cupboard,
constantly mesmerized
by your faded voice.

I cried when you cared for me,
and I trembled with fear
that I broke up the message
I was honored to carry for you.
Can you see my tormented soul?

I came to believe
that your love was mine forever,
so I turned over
my wounded ego to you.
You commanded me to inventory
my demons and Angels,
and then let you decide.

This conversation transformed
who I thought I was,
and I quickly took leave on the glass boat,
along the river of fire,
that was waiting for me.
Our long talks late into the night,
brought me my own recovered heart

on a silver platter,
and I continued to worship you.

You would not know
how I filled myself up with you,
kicking out anything
other than your beautiful, broken self.

I mistakenly thought I would die
if you did not continue
to breathe in my direction.

I worshipped a human being,
and my soul mourned her loss of me.

You would not know of any of this,
because you continue to circle
your broken mirrors.

I tried desperately to get your attention,
but you were seeking those who cannot see you.
I continue to fall into your heart,
ripping up the floorboards,
proving that I can still save you.
I cried and ran to my community
of mothers and fathers,
hoping that God would forgive how lost I became.

Slowly, and with my heart
drying out from all the blood
that was spilled running after you,
I began to hear God whispering the solution.
I tried to share God's invitation with you,

but it had only my name on it.
You still rejected me,
and this rejection became a life-long trap
of needless suffering.

And this is why I still write you these letters.
I know that you are reading them,
and that you too,
have filled your emptiness
with men and women who wear masks.

All of their masks threw you into the pit
of faulty, broken promises
for salvation, redemption and torment,
your ultimate distraction: Obsessive Love.
I know all of this
because I too have worn these masks,
and worshipped those who wore them.

Now I just stand in front of you,
not with any mask,
but with my vulnerabilities.
Is not this what you asked of me?

How you shamelessly spoke of my secrets,
loudly so all the souls of dead poets past
can hear you
and murmur their agreement with you?

I bare my vulnerabilities for you,
in the hope that one day you will write me back,
and say that you can still hear
my heart beating for you.

But that this beating sings to a rhythm of God
who saved me, forgave me, and gently guides me
to continue seeking you.

"Who are you that God wants you to seek?"
you may ask yourself.

I will return with my answer,
after the sun has set upon us,
and you forever promise me your heart.

I STAYED UP ALL NIGHT
STARING AT YOUR PHOTOGRAPH

I heard you calling to my heart last night.
I could not help it...staring at your photograph
all night long,
my heart pounding at the excitement
that one day we will be reunited again.

I know you gaze at my photo too,
because that is when I feel your cries
running rivers along my chest;
sadness and grief beyond words.

I lit a candle and said a prayer,
hoping to soften the grip
your voice still has on me.

You came to tell me that a bond of real love
has no ending.
Hour after long hour,
deep into the night,
I felt you wrap your heart around me,
and I felt your hand in mine.

From miles and miles away,
sometimes your voice is faint,
and other times it is so strong
that the candle blows itself out.

This is how I know for sure
that we still hear each other,
that we touch each other

from many moons away.

You never ran away
and I never hid.
That was only our frightened and bruised egos
yearning for the Great Mother to feed us.

I have learned through you,
and because of you,
that this Great Being that exists
and from where we come,
wrote it in the stars long ago,
that you and I would forever
be one of the same.

And so I sit here alone,
on top of this regal mountain,
gazing at the patient moon,
and writing you this letter.

Sooner than we expect,
I will come down to the village
and I will look for you.

When we reunite,
we will only know of a fire
that extended far beyond
what we could have created
with our egos alone.

You were right back then,
that the Sun did not shine upon our union,
that the time and circumstances

did not invite our love.

But now you can feel this love coming closer,
can't you?

If you read this letter,
will you draw me a heart on the sand,
on the exact spot we stood
when we tried to free
our broken, wounded hearts
from each other's ravaging egos?

I will know when you have done so,
just like I have absorbed
every tear you cried for me
during this long exile
from each other.

Then kiss my name across the ocean,
and I will never let it leave
my heart's pathways.

Will you?

MY VALENTINE'S DAY GIFT

I have successfully battled my way
out of a deep slumber
of a once life preserving,
intoxicating fog
of denial, lies, and enabling deception.

It has been such a successful rescue operation,
that I almost forgot how to empathize
with those who choose to remain
in the snake's den.
Almost.
But I have no patience for those
who massage their lies
in order to feel alive.

Such people will inadvertently
be a seductive spokesperson for the snake
that wishes to invite my innocence
back to its dark den of faulty attachments.

This decision is my ultimate gift of love to myself.

FADED CHILDREN'S VOICES ON THE MERRY-GO-ROUND: THE LAST PAGE IN THIS NOTEBOOK

As children we learn to fly
with our childlike passions.
We sing, dance, twirl, laugh,
love and cry with the freedom
of the most graceful of beings.

The younger the child,
the more possessive they are
of their love object.
It is a love that is fierce and intense,
lacking the futile insecurities
and drama of adulthood.

This is because children do not mix
anything less than fulfillment
into their magical way of being.
Then life calls,
and the child grows into an adult,
learning all of society's rules
for what is now called "love",
but understood very differently
by the once-innocent child.

Sadness may set in,
as the adult learns that to let go
is to give space for their adult love object
to awaken.
And in that space is the frightening risk
that perhaps the adult was not loved

as they thought they were.

That being loved was confused with need,
lust, self-centered fulfillment of desires, and so on.

How different are the rules of this new game,
as we watch our childhood passion crumble
into a slowly fading heap of ashes.

Some people give up entirely;
some keep up
in a desperate, demoralizing search
for that "perfect, magical love",
never stopping to investigate anything at all.

And some, remain terribly hopeful
and avoidant at the same time.

We all have this struggle
as part of our basic, flawed, imperfect humanity.
This is what makes us seekers,
and what drives the poets, artists and philosophers
to keep the quest and conversation going.

Our transformation occurs
when we learn how to be courageous enough
to be vulnerable, to uncover the masks we don
to protect our sensitive souls.

Perhaps a life changing event, tragedy,
or heartbreak pushes us to examine and discover
that we have deeply rooted pain
with what we call "love".

But if we listen closely
to the faded voices of our childhood,
we will no longer have to cry
for those who left us.

We now know and believe
that true love always was,
and always will be,
our birthright.

It is not up to someone else
to find us earning and deserving,
that we do not have to wait
until our self-esteem is complete enough
for us to receive love.

If we keep our conversation going
between our wounds,
and this magical force called Love,
we will give voice to our hearts.

A holy triangle of three
will transform our lives
if we allow ourselves to be guided
by their sacred conversation.

As a final note,
I wish to thank you, my beloved reader,
for taking the time to read this notebook
of love, song, and poetry.

I had you in mind when I wrote it,

227

hoping that by reading
and taking these words to heart,
you will have the courage to be vulnerable,
to love from that place,
and to spread your courage
to every person who still remains asleep.

Will you join me on this sacred journey?